The Analytic Encounter

Marie-Louise von Franz, Honorary Patron

**Studies in Jungian Psychology
by Jungian Analysts**

Daryl Sharp, General Editor

The
Analytic
Encounter

Transference and Human Relationship

Mario Jacoby

Canadian Cataloguing in Publication Data
Jacoby, Mario, 1925-
The analytic encounter

(Studies in Jungian psychology by Jungian analysts; 15)

Bibliography: p.
Includes index.

ISBN 0-919123-14-7

1. Psychotherapist and patient. 2. Transference (Psychology). I. Title. II. Series.

RC480.8.J32 1984   616.89'17   C84-098258-5

INNER CITY BOOKS
Box 1271, Station Q, Toronto, Canada M4T 2P4
Telephone (416) 927-0355

Honorary Patron: Marie-Louise von Franz.
Publisher and General Editor: Daryl Sharp.
Editorial Board: Fraser Boa, Daryl Sharp, Marion Woodman.

INNER CITY BOOKS was founded in 1980 to promote the understanding and practical application of the work of C.G. Jung.

Cover: "The Naked Truth," alchemical image used by C.G. Jung to characterize the essentially spiritual significance of the transference relationship (see text, pages 106-108).

Photo page 45 courtesy Jessie (left) and Vicki.

Glossary and Index by Daryl Sharp.

Printed and bound in Canada by
University of Toronto Press Incorporated

Contents

See last pages for descriptions of other INNER CITY BOOKS

Alchemical image of the *coniunctio* (union of opposites) as fountain, symbol for the meaningful flow of life. (*Rosarium philsophorum*, 1550)

Preface

Another book on transference? Is this really necessary, considering the abundance of material already available?

I believe it is, particularly because most of the writing on transference has been done by analysts of the Freudian school of thought, conceived within the framework of psychoanalytic theory and technique. It is intended primarily for "insiders" and is described in very abstract, scientific terminology. I do appreciate their work. Freudian psychoanalysts are admittedly less interested in describing the experience of transference than in explaining it in terms of an overall metapsychological theory, and professional therapists may well profit from their research without accepting all of their theoretical assumptions.

My concern here, however, is with the actual human experiences that are part and parcel of psychic life—the feelings, sufferings, passions and frustrations—and how these may manifest in the analytic encounter. My hope is to enable the educated layman, as well as the professional, to truly grasp the impact of the phenomena termed transference and counter-transference on those in therapy.

My aim is therefore to communicate to the reader how the interactions going on between analyst and analysand may feel —or, at least, how they often feel to me. I am interested in both the everyday problems of analytic practice, and in the archetypal depth-dimension—discovered by C.G. Jung—that lies behind the "banalities" of personal involvements.

The material here was originally presented in the form of a lecture series, and this unacademic style and tone have been preserved. The main purpose is not to give technical hints on "how to treat transference problems," nor to give a comprehensive account of the differing theories on the subject in modern depth psychology. Rather I am concerned with promoting an enhanced sensitivity to the psychological subtleties involved in any human encounter, and especially those in the intimate relationship that develops in analysis.

I want to thank my analysands who gave permission to publish their material. For reasons of discretion all personal details that are not relevant have been omitted or altered. My thanks are due also to the trainees at the C.G. Jung Institute in Zurich and to many professional audiences in Brazil, Germany, Israel and the United States, whose stimulating and thought-provoking responses to my lectures and seminars have been a continuous help in clarifying my ideas.

I am particularly grateful to Eleanor Mattern for editing my manuscript with sensitivity and empathy.

Introduction

The psychological relationship between analyst and patient or analysand, so central to any therapeutic activity, is relatively neglected in the practice and literature of Jungians. A prominent exception is the work of the London school of analytical psychology inspired by Michael Fordham, in which clinical interest is directed almost exclusively to the observation and interpretation of the so-called transference and countertransference.[1] There is also the research on transference published by Jungian analysts in Berlin in the early seventies.[2] But in general there is greater interest among Jungians in material from the unconscious (dreams, drawings, etc.) than in the interrelations of analyst and analysand.

This may be due partially to the fact that Jung himself seemed to minimize the importance of the transference after his break in 1912 with Freud. One can find many statements that even seem to show that he felt transference was unimportant. These appear mainly in his lectures at the Tavistock Clinic in London in 1935, where he said:

> A transference is always a hindrance; it is never an advantage. You cure in spite of the transference, not because of it. . . .
>
> Transference or no transference, that has nothing to do with the cure. . . . If there is no transference, so much the better. You get the material just the same. It is not transference that enables the patient to bring out his material; you get all the material you could wish for from dreams. The dreams bring out everything that is necessary.[3]

Here Jung clearly overstates his point, as may be seen in light of his later, more considered views. Indeed, we shall also see that sometimes the transference actually influences dreams —if not their content, at least the way in which the dream is interpreted and its message integrated.

Jung's remarks in his Tavistock lectures must be understood in their context. He had wanted to continue a discussion of dream material and its amplification, but his audience was mainly medical doctors and they wanted to hear his views on transference. We can sense a certain irritation in him when he agrees to discuss "the half-amusing, half-painful, even tragic problems of transference,"[4] but he goes on to make some very significant points.

One of his main ideas is that transference has to be considered as a lack of real human relationship, "a difficulty in making contact, in establishing emotional harmony between the doctor and the patient."[5] Transference feelings arise in order to compensate for this lack of rapport. Therefore he states:

> When you really try to be on a level with the patient, not too high nor too low, when you have the right attitude, the right appreciation, then you have much less trouble with the transference. It won't save you from it entirely, but sure enough you won't have those bad forms of transference which are mere over-compensation for a lack of rapport.[6]

Here Jung rightly distinguishes between transference and an entirely human feeling relationship between analyst and analysand. This idea, that transference is an overcompensation for a lack of real human relationship, derives from Jung's view that transference is a particular form of projection, which tends to falsify any relationship. Hence the maturing or individuation process is typically marked by a transformation of transference feelings (withdrawal of projections). In making these observations it is of course necessary to arrive at a certain clarity in distinguishing transference and countertransference from what may properly be called genuine relationship or rapport. This is a central issue that will be discussed in detail in the course of this book.

Jung's main contribution to the theme of this book, however, is his long essay called "The Psychology of the Transference."[7] Here he obviously appreciates the central place transference holds in a deep analysis, for he writes:

> It is probably no exaggeration to say that almost all cases requiring lengthy treatment gravitate round the phenomenon of transference, and that the success or failure of the treatment appears to be bound up with it in a very fundamental way.[8]

In this work Jung chose to interpret the transference in conjunction with a set of illustrations from the alchemical text,

Rosarium philosophorum (1550)—or perhaps he was already in inner dialogue with these symbolic expressions of what the alchemists called the mystical marriage or *coniunctio*. It is in any case an impressive example of Jung's attempt to avoid abstract terminology when dealing with psychic experience. As he writes elsewhere:

> In describing the living processes of the psyche, I deliberately and consciously give preference to a dramatic, mythological way of thinking and speaking, because this is not only more expressive but also more exact than an abstract scientific terminology, which is wont to toy with the notion that its theoretic formulations may one fine day be resolved into algebraic equations.[9]

The content of Jung's essay is rich and tremendously stimulating, and I shall indeed refer to it in the course of this book. Yet for the psychotherapist it is rather difficult to draw from it a feeling for how to handle transference and countertransference in an ordinary daily practice. Jung did not in fact intend his essay "for the beginner who would first have to be instructed in such matters," and explicitly states that "the reader will not find an account of the clinical phenomena of transference."[10]

I believe, however, that it is important for an analyst to consider himself each day "a beginner," so that he continually questions what is happening between himself and his analysands. This is in line with Jung's statement that "each new case that requires thorough treatment is pioneer work, and every trace of routine then proves to be a blind alley."[11] More than once he cautioned one to be always open to the uniqueness of each living psyche; for instance:

> Theories in psychology are the very devil. It is true that we need certain points of view for their orienting and heuristic value; but they should always be regarded as mere auxiliary concepts that can be laid aside at any time. We still know so very little about the psyche that it is positively grotesque to think we are far enough advanced to frame general theories. No doubt theory is the best cloak for lack of experience and ignorance, but the consequences are depressing: bigotedness, superficiality, and scientific sectarianism.[12]

His own experience, he wrote,

> has taught me to keep away from therapeutic "methods" as much as from diagnoses. The enormous variation among individuals and their neuroses has set before me the ideal of approaching each case with a minimum of prior assumptions. The ideal would naturally be to have no assumptions at all.[13]

Jung knew, of course, that this was not possible ("for one is *oneself* the biggest of all one's assumptions, and the one with the gravest consequences"),[14] but he strongly encouraged his students to find their own way:

> I can only hope and wish that no one becomes "Jungian." ... I proclaim no cut-and-dried doctrine, and I abhor "blind adherents." I leave everyone free to deal with the facts in his own way, since I also claim this freedom for myself.[15]

It is in this spirit of exploration that I present what follows: my experience and understanding of psychic reality as I have encountered it—in myself, in my analysands and in the field of our mutual relationship.

1

The Analytic Encounter

The practice of Jungian psychotherapy consists of two persons
meeting in order to try to understand what is going on in the
unconscious of one of them. The patient or analysand usually
has symptoms, conflicts or other deep dissatisfactions with
which he has been struggling by himself in vain, for they seem
to be more powerful than any conscious will power at his
disposal. He therefore needs help and comes to a psychotherapist. The source of his neurosis, narcissistic personality disorder, borderline state, etc., is hidden from both patient and
analyst; together they explore unconscious causes, aims and
meanings.

In this work the analyst tends to place much emphasis on
dreams, trying to understand them and link them to the patient's life-history and especially to his conscious standpoint.
But how does the patient experience this assistance? Who is
the analyst for the patient?

If we want to explore the unconscious, it is not only of the
utmost importance to investigate what is going on between the
conscious situation of the patient and the unconscious responses or compensations depicted in dreams. Sooner or later it
will also become important to consider what is going on between the two persons involved in this process. The so-called
analytic relationship between the partners is absolutely necessary for a therapeutic process, but some aspects of it further
this process and others tend to hinder it. The analytic encounter can become as complex as any intimate relationship. Unconscious fantasies stemming from vital needs tend to arise
between the partners. Sometimes they are not intense but
quite subtle, and thus escape being noticed at all by either
analyst or patient. Yet they may influence the analysis by
causing resistances, provoking strong illusions about the analyst or the patient, or tending to sexualize the relationship.

All this is well known by now, and the technical term for

these unconscious projections is transference or countertransference, depending on the direction of the projections.

The analytic relationship, however, is not identical with what we call transference and countertransference. Although there are those who would see all the interactions between analytic partners in such terms, as a matter of fact we also find real human relationship in the therapeutic situation. There are, as mentioned already, many places in the writings of Jung which show that he saw a difference between transference and human relationship in the analytic situation. I consider it of the greatest importance to increase our sensitivity to what is going on between the partners in analysis. Transference can hide itself behind apparently real human relationship; or sometimes what is interpreted as transference is really genuine human relationship. What is the difference between these two attitudes which are called transference and human relationship? What are the implications of these phenomena for the subtleties of the analytic situation?

The purpose of this book is to offer some answers to these questions, but first let us consider what the two pioneers in depth psychology understood by transference.

Freud's Views on Transference

To Sigmund Freud must go the credit for first discovering the phenomenon of transference in psychoanalysis. Together with Josef Breuer, his first attempt to reach unconscious material was by means of hypnosis. In the state of hypnosis the patient could recall memories of early childhood he had forgotten or repressed.

Hypnosis seemed at first to be a perfect new method for getting at psychic trauma; recalling the traumatic event usually had a healing effect upon the hysteric patient. Freud never used hypnotic *suggestion*. He did not suggest to the patient in his hypnotic state a more positive attitude because he did not want the will of the doctor to influence the patient. Such influence he considered not genuine and of only temporary value, and therefore he used hypnosis purely to get at forgotten childhood memories.

Although it seemed at first to Freud and Breuer that this

method was optimal, they found out fairly soon that many patients could not respond to it but resisted the attempts of the therapist to hypnotize them. Thus Freud was led to the discovery that resistance was part of the whole neurotic structure and was connected with the fear of recalling shameful and painful memories. From this insight he developed his theories of neurosis.

But Freud also discovered another cause of resistance to the therapist's attempts to hypnotize—namely, any disturbance in the relationship between patient and doctor. In his "Studies on Hysteria" (1895), Freud mentions three possible reasons for the disturbance of this relationship.[16] First, the patient may feel that the doctor does not take him seriously enough, or neglects him or ridicules his innermost secrets. It also may be that the patient has heard negative judgments about his doctor or his way of treatment. Second, the case may arise, especially with women, that a patient fears the loss of her independence through falling into a psychic and even sexual dependence on the therapist. As a third cause for a disturbed doctor-patient relationship, Freud mentions the fact that patients tend to get a shock when they discover the "transference" of shameful fantasies onto the person of the doctor.

Here the term transference appears for the first time, and Freud gives the following now-famous example to show what he means by it. After the termination of an analytic session a woman patient of his suddenly felt an intense wish that Freud would give her a kiss. Of course she did not mention it at the time; she was disgusted with herself for having such a thought, and spent a sleepless night. During the next session she was very disturbed and blocked in her associations until she had mentioned this fantasy. Freud tried to find out the cause of this wish-fantasy and came to the conclusion that the source for it was an experience which had happened to the patient many years ago. At that time she had had a talk with a man, during which she had noticed—and repressed—the sudden wish that this man might force a kiss upon her. Now this wish had come up again, "transferred" from its real object to the therapist.[17] In this way Freud found out that unsatisfied or repressed wishes of the past tend to get transferred to a new object, namely the analyst.

At first this new discovery disturbed him, as he saw his method of psychoanalysis getting more and more complicated. But after a while he came to the conclusion that the occurrence of transference had many advantages for the healing process. It reactivated repressed childhood wishes and experiences and thus led to the core of the neurosis. This discovery of transference-love was a shock less to Freud than to his collaborator Breuer, who subsequently gave up psychoanalysis altogether, mainly because he took the love personally and could not bear it.[18]

Freud continued to study the phenomenon of transference, and more and more came to the opinion that it was in fact *necessary* for any successful psychoanalytic cure, as he called his therapy. Patients who were not able to fall into transference were not treatable by psychoanalysis. The forms of neurosis which tended to show transference-reactions when dealt with were conversion-hysteria, phobia and compulsion neurosis. These three forms were therefore treatable by classical psychoanalysis, and Freud called them transference neuroses.

Transference onto the therapist of infantile love-expectations, as well as repressed hatred and aggression, was for Freud the condition for successful treatment. On the other hand, it was exactly the transference which seemed, according to Freud, to sabotage quick healing; the original neurosis transformed itself during analysis to a new kind of neurosis, which he called again transference neurosis. In other words, the patient gets tied to the analyst and this dependence can remove him from all personal responsibility. He can feel himself to be the beloved infant of the analyst-father or mother and unconsciously does not want to give up this dependence. The healing of his neurosis would mean at the same time giving up his dependence on the analyst, and therefore he unconsciously refuses to get better. Thus transference can also cause a resistance against the healing process.

What advice does Freud give to the analyst for dealing with this state of affairs? How can the analyst help his patient to overcome this so-called transference-resistance? Here the famous "abstinence rule" comes in. This means that the analyst should not give any emotional response to the demands put upon him by the patient, except for the interpretation of motives. The analyst should remain as cool as a surgeon undertaking an operation.[19]

This keeping-out of emotional response is, in Freud's view, for the benefit of the patient; at the same time he mentions that this attitude of objective, free-floating attention is also a protection for the emotional life of the analyst. Why is this cool, unresponsive attitude of the analyst to the benefit of the patient? Because transference is a form of neurosis, a wish to stay dependent on the doctor and not to become independent. Therefore any demand of the patient which is fulfilled by the analyst keeps the patient longer in dependence.

The job of the analyst, then, consists only and purely in interpreting the motives causing this dependence called transference. And the motives behind the transference seem clear to Freud. Demands and wishes whose gratification the patient seeks from the analyst are in reality repetitions of early childhood needs and conflicts. In his relationship to the analyst the patient repeats and relives the love, hatred, aggression and frustration he experienced as an infant in relation to his parents. The interpretation of transference behavior and fantasies consists therefore of showing the patient that his love or hate for the analyst is not something real and basic, that his feelings do not come out of the present situation but repeat former experiences, mostly of early infancy.

These interpretations aim at an important psychotherapeutic process, namely the transformation of *repetitions* into *memories*.[20] Leading the patient to insight into his early fixations serves the healing aim of becoming conscious and dealing with those difficulties in an adult way. By this means the dependence called transference to the analyst can be overcome.

If we listen to Freud we get a clear-cut theory about the phenomenon of transference: early childhood experiences get transferred to the analyst, and the emotions and feelings involved are only repetitions of the original ones. We also get a technique for dealing with the transference: interpretation of motives with the aim of transforming the repetitions into memories. The abstinence rule forbidding any involvement on the part of the analyst makes sense in this context. The technique of treatment is a logical consequence of the whole

Freudian theory about the psyche and the occurrence of transference.

I think it is important to keep these first observations on transference phenomena in mind. They form a historical framework within which one may better understand Jung's starting-point. And after all there is much truth in them, and they give a valuable and most necessary point of view in any analysis.

The Contribution of C.G. Jung

Freud's straightforward, purely causalistic theory was for Jung too narrow and one-sided. Two main factors seemed to Jung to be neglected in the Freudian view.

First, Freud was concerned only with the *cause* of transference—he asked what caused this strange dependence, the transference neurosis. Jung thought that transference was an entirely natural occurrence in any relationship, and so it also happens often—though not always—during analysis. It must therefore have not only a cause but also a purpose. He became interested in the question of what *meaning* the transference might have.

Second, Freud believed that transference was a repetition of repressed childhood experiences. This would mean that only material from the personal life-history, the personal unconscious, would be involved in it. But in such a deep, frequently occurring and important phenomenon as transference, one would expect that archetypal contents from the collective unconscious would also come into play. In *Two Essays on Analytical Psychology* (1928), Jung describes a case where the dreams of a patient who had an intense transference to Jung showed clearly that unconsciously the analyst meant god, a spiritual, divine being, for her. Jung saw this as a projection of the Self—the archetype of wholeness and the regulating center of the psyche—onto the analyst. The patient was tied to and dependent on the analyst as long as she had not realized the projected content in herself, that is, her own center.[21]

I think also of a case of mine. The patient came to the analytic hour in an angry mood because the previous week things went wrong for him: a girl whom he seemed to love left him. He was angry with me, his analyst, because he felt that I denied him the pleasure of having and loving a girl, and that therefore fate was bad to him. On the other hand, of course, he knew that I had nothing to do directly with the breaking of his relationship with the girl. All the same, the irrational idea had taken hold of him that I should have intervened in the form of Venus—or at least her son Eros—and shot some love-arrows at the girl at the last moment. The patient did not let this fantasy come to consciousness at first because of its ab-surdity, but felt only intense anger. He knew that I had noth-ing to do with this break, that I was only trying, together with him, to find out why girls always left him after a certain time. Nevertheless, he got in a rage about his fate, and took it out on me; he quarreled with me as one quarrels with a god.

At this period the patient was so dependent on me that he always wanted advice for everything, or at least a later absolu-tion once he had done something. There was more in this transference than just an ordinary father-projection, for un-consciously he bestowed superhuman power on me. He also thought that I knew the outcome of everything and was cruel because I did not tell him—for it was clear to him that if I was the master of his fate, I must already know everything in advance. This is only one example to show how archetypal contents may be activated in a transference situation.

Now if unconscious archetypal contents are involved in the transference, it follows that the motives behind the transfer-ence cannot be only a repetition of personal life-situations. In the unconscious we find also the seeds of further develop-ment, which may be brought to the attention of consciousness and gradually integrated with it. Transference is really a form of projection; in fact, the term transference is just the English translation of the Latin *projectio,* "projection." We use the word transference as a technical term for the projections oc-curring in the patient-analyst relationship. According to Jung, we speak of projection when psychic contents belonging to subjective, intrapsychic experiences are experienced in the outer world in relation to other people or objects. This means we are not conscious that these contents are really part of our own psychic structure.

Some patients, for instance, will quite often say to me such

things as: "I know exactly what you think now, I can feel it—
you think that my behavior is terribly immoral, you think that
I am just no good," when I am really not conscious of any
such thoughts. This kind of criticism is a basic problem for
these patients. They are not aware that these judgments take
place in themselves, that the negative self-criticism is projected
onto the outer world and, of course, onto the analyst. They
think that the analyst surely has negative thoughts about them
although of course he cannot admit as much—the treatment
needs a lot of psychological tricks, and so forth.

Of course, the observation of *what* contents get projected
gives important clues to the analyst, showing in which areas
growing consciousness is vitally needed for the patient. The
projected contents are not only repetitions uncovering repressed material. New contents of the creative psyche may
come up and are experienced first in projection. Thus the
inner process of self-realization, the process Jung called *individuation,* is very often at work behind the specific coloring,
contents and forms that a transference shows.[22] This is one of
Jung's most important insights into this strange phenomenon.
And, of course, from this point of view, dealing with it becomes very complex. Rules and techniques for dealing with
transference have thus lost their ground. The Jungian analyst
is often faced with most delicate and difficult, yet sometimes
rewarding, transference situations.

A Case Example

A twenty-three-year-old, extremely inhibited woman brought
after the first analytical session the following initial dream:

> I am in a house. There is an elderly man who wants to murder
> me and cuts open my arteries. I call for help and try to dress
> the wounds myself. Then I am able to escape and look for a
> doctor. The man follows me. In the end I am with the doctor,
> who binds up the wounds.

From her associations it was clear that this persecuting
murderer represented an attitude she had experienced from
her mother, and which became destructively effective and
powerful inside herself. According to her description, her
mother was a domineering, pious Catholic who tried from

early on to convey to her children that a righteous life is saying prayers and fulfilling one's duties. She was suffering from a nervous heart condition and used this heart trouble for power purposes. If her children or husband resisted her, she fell ill and thus constellated guilt feelings in them.

My very sensitive patient was depressive and showed many of those symptoms which usually arise from a disturbed primal relationship and a lack of primary trust.[23] Her behavior toward her mother had from early on been rebellious, essentially healthy. But her rebellion was invariably followed by guilt feelings and remorse. She then had to apologize to mother and mother forgave generously. Rebellion was a sin which had to be forgiven by mother and later by her father confessor in church. My patient could not of course see the utmost importance of her rebellious impulses and thus could not trust her own feelings. She became more and more cut off from her own nature and increasingly dependent on mother.

Jürg Willi, a Swiss psychoanalyst, says that the child of a mother suffering from a narcissistic disorder has to live from early on with the following paradox: I am only myself if I fulfil the expectations mother has of me. If, however, I am as I feel, then I am *not* myself.[24] My analysand's unconscious feeling that she had no right to live her own life according to her own nature was expressed in the initial dream by her arteries being cut. In terms of the Jungian model the murderous old man would represent her mother's negative animus, now internalized.

With this problem she came to the doctor, presumably a healthy reaction to her inability to help herself. It seems that after the first hour she felt I had treated her "wound" adequately. Soon an intense and very complex transference developed, characterized by one particularly important incident: One day she brought a dream in which I had given her Jung's book on the divine child. After she had told me this dream, I went to my bookshelf and gave her the book to read. That was my spontaneous reaction, an impulse to which I gave in and which felt all right at the time. Of course, this reaction might be questioned. Some analysts might have preferred to get into her fantasies connected with the divine child and also with the fact that I, the analyst, gave her that book in the dream. I spontaneously chose the concretization—the acting-out, so to speak—of the dream-fantasy. Naturally I wondered how she was going to react to it and thought there would be time to go into her fantasies in the next session.

The next time she came she apologized in distress that she was just not able to read the book because she hated it from the first line. She added that surely she was just too stupid to understand it, and again apologized. I sensed a mixed reaction within myself. I definitely could spot a feeling of disappoint-ment that this book did not have a better effect on her and that she had to reject something which I thought valuable and therapeutically meaningful. I felt even an impulse of anger. Yet my inner reaction of disappointment and anger was mel-lowed by her excuses and her self-devaluation.

I thought again of her initial dream, in which the destruc-tive man follows her to the doctor's office. On the one hand, an important process had started in her unconscious, a process to which the meaningful symbolism of the divine child re-ferred (as I saw also in later dreams). On the other hand, it was also evident that she had begun to repeat with me the pattern of rebellion and forgiveness she had experienced with her mother. It seemed that I, as her analyst, received not only the projection of the helping doctor but also of the murderous animus.

This complicated matters considerably. After all, she had dreamt I gave her that important book. This wish was surely directed at the doctor and had a deep meaning in relation to her inner development. But my giving her the book meant at the same time, to her, that I was saying: Look here, this is what you *should* read, this *should* be of concern to you and not something else, this is the way you *ought to* handle your inner child—all in the critical language that is typical of a negative animus. It was very important for her to revolt against that inner figure, which had become transferred onto me. But rebellion constellated intense guilt feelings and there-fore she had to excuse herself again and again. Really allow-ing herself that rebellion was from one point of view more important than reading the book, therefore I did not go into her resistance to the dream, but interpreted her behavior as a repetition of her rebellion-and-repair pattern. I also remarked that her rebellion was healthy and represented her tendency toward independence. I could see that this interpretation was a great relief to her.

Yet after all, she really had dreamed that I was giving her the book, and I also wanted to talk with her about that. Seen in the context of her dream, everything looked different again. She admitted that at first she had felt more than pleased when I gave her the book. It meant that I was taking her dreams very seriously, as an important part of herself. She also experienced my belief that she would be capable of reading such a book as a great affirmation. Since early childhood, she had had fantasies about a knowing man with experience of life and complete understanding of all her inner turmoils. She said that when she came to the first analytical session, she knew that I was the man of her fantasies—and then immediately added, "But all this is just ridiculous and terribly exaggerated. And anyhow I am much too stupid to read such a book."

Here you can see how the destructive animus got into action again as a resistance to the doctor and the healing tendencies in herself. In reality her mother had always reproached her with living in the clouds and exaggerating everything and told her that it was high time to become "reasonable."

It seems to me that in this situation I represented on the one hand the knowing man of her fantasy who understood and supported her inner life—exactly *in contrast to* her mother. On the other hand, she was always afraid that I would criticize or ridicule her if she exposed herself and that I expected her to be reasonable—just *like* her mother. Now, if she experienced me as the knowing healer, not reading the book surely had to be seen as resistance to her own inner healing process. But if I represented the negative animus, not reading the book then had to do with healthy rebellion for the sake of her own growth. Her transference thus showed both the repetition of her interactions with the personal mother and the unconscious projection of what may be called the wise healer archetype.

Understanding the complexity of such a transference does not mean that it is necessarily easier to arrive at an adequate therapeutic response. As already mentioned, I interpreted the transference of her mother's negative animus in a so-called reductive way, especially to get her connected with memories of similar interactions which evoked similar emotions. But what about the constellation of the healer archetype in the transference? Her vital need to be understood and taken seriously had apparently created this archetypal fantasy-figure at quite an early age. The patient was in reality an introverted feeling type. Behind the surface of shyness, inhibition and apparent lack of contact her psyche was intensely alive and she was full of questions concerning the meaning of life. Her connection to this essential side in herself was constantly disrupted by the voice of the destructive animus, which told her that it was ridiculous to take such unreal ideas seriously. But the wise man with his life-experience understood everything that was of such vital concern to her soul. This fantasy was decisive, as it helped her to trust her inner values and to allow their manifestations.

In the event, I felt that the transference of this archetypal figure was not something to be immediately interpreted. Rather, it was important to allow it as a living experience, even if in reality, of course, I might have to beware of the subtle temptation to see myself as such a wise and ideal figure. Sometimes an analyst cannot help but incarnate an archetype, so to speak. The disappointing realization that the analyst is just an ordinary human being has to come gradually and not by a traumatic shock. One has to allow for the slow process of taking back projections: the projected content may then be recognized by the analysand as intrapsychic and can be partially integrated.

In this woman's dream it seemed that I, as the figure of the wise healer, wanted to help her connect with the divine child, that is, the child in herself, with all its manifold symbolism. This surely also had to do with making contact with memories and fantasies of her childhood, when the spontaneous manifestation of her true nature had been inhibited.

2

Transference and Countertransference

The Jungian Model

The following diagram shows the complexity of what is going on psychologically between two persons in the analytic relationship. It is a variation of Jung's drawing in "The Psychology of the Transference," inspired by what he calls the marriage quaternio, which he used to illustrate the various relationships between a man and a woman or patient and analyst.[25] For my purposes I have slightly altered his drawing, so that it can serve as a model for all kinds of transference configurations between analysts and patients of the same sex or of opposite sex.[26]

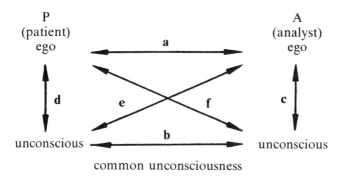

common unconsciousness

This model is useful in describing what typically happens in a deep analysis. The patient (P) comes for consultation to the analyst (A). P has certain difficulties or symptoms and wants to be free of them, wants to be cured. The analyst might tell him that psychotherapy depends mainly on mutual cooperation between P and A, in contrast to somatic medicine where chemotherapy works by itself or where one has to endure an operation passively. P has to pay a good deal of money for the analysis, and one would assume that he wants to do his best to

25

help the treatment. If both feel it would be worthwhile to give psychotherapy a try, P and A agree to cooperate and form a conscious relationship to discuss P's difficulties (line **a**).

This is all very well, but the situation often becomes more complex. The agreement to cooperate was made mainly by the ego of P and the ego of A, but both have their unconscious sides. Suppose the unconscious of P reacts to A (line **e**). He may look forward to the appointment with A, find that the discussions mean something to him, and feel relieved after the hour and safe in the relationship—or there may be anxieties: he does not like A, hates him for having to talk about disagreeable or painful things, or fears A might make fun of him or reject him if he gets to know shameful secrets. He feels confidence in A, or he mistrusts him. P may fear—especially, but not only, if A and P are of opposite sexes—that he or she might fall in love and become completely dependent on A. This prospect arouses anxiety and may be at the same time a wish. Very often P behaves and reacts to A as he does generally to all persons with whom he has a close relationship.

All this means that P expresses to A more or less intense emotions which belong in general not to A but to the experiences of P. A has therefore the possibility of entering to a certain extent into the unconscious of P by means of so-called active projection (empathy),[27] feeling his way into the emotional and fantasy life of P. A wants, of course, to establish a relationship both to the ego and to the unconscious of P (lines **a** and **e**) and thus help P get in contact with his own soul (line **d**). A cannot in fact interpret a dream or any other aspect of P's life in an effective way without entering into P's whole situation—the conflicts, links and compensations between P's conscious ego and P's unconscious.

Now A too has some feelings as a result of the contact with P. He might find him a nice and valuable person and want to try and help him, or find him a bore, full of superficial nonsense, without the slightest bit of imagination or wit. P may seem to A to be agreeable and good-looking, or coarse, ugly and disagreeable. A gets ideas about the present state of P and about the way he ought to change. For instance, he would just like to shake him out of his passivity; or he thinks that P should finally just have the courage to sleep with a woman; or he thinks that P should dress more nicely and certainly go to a hairdresser. A must always be very careful when that little word "should" comes up. Maybe P "should" be different simply to fit the image that A unconsciously has of him. Or A gives a lot of special attention to P just because P loves and adores him; or P is hardly to be tolerated when he shows disagreeable resistance against A, indicating that A has the need to be loved and adored by his patient; or A is very disappointed when P does not show any improvement through treatment.

In fact the whole diagnosis as well as the interpretations and evaluations of P's material are based on the feelings and perceptions of A. And here we come to the tricky question: Does A really see P in an adequate light? Do A's evaluations, expectations and feelings correspond to the psychic reality of P, or does A project his own unconscious contents upon P (line f)? Who decides about *this?*

Jung's awareness of this problem was one of the main reasons why he demanded a thorough analysis of the analyst. In fact he was the first to do so, and it was on Jung's suggestion that Freud saw the importance of the so-called training analysis. Now it is compulsory in virtually every school of depth psychology. *Theoretically* the training analysis lessens the danger of wild projections from the side of the analyst because through it he becomes more conscious of what happens in himself. An increased awareness of his complexes, his weaknesses, his principles of evaluation and his personal standpoint or *Weltanschauung* is vitally important for his job, for there can be disastrous results if he projects those on P.

Of course, no training analysis, no matter how thorough, can prevent one completely from projecting. There are always blind spots and unconscious areas as long as we live, hence the countertransference, the inevitability that A will from time to time project unconscious contents onto P. Often P's remarks or behavior just hit a soft or weak spot in A; sometimes P has exactly the main complex that A suffers from. But with some effort and honesty they might still work very well together for the benefit of both.

Perhaps one of the most important qualities for A to have is his readiness to question his point of view, his reactions, feelings, emotions and thoughts again and again in new situations, without losing his spontaneity. He must be aware of the constant possibility of projections from his side. For myself, I know that if problems of my patients bother me in an autonomous way, if "it thinks in me" about a certain patient, then I am caught in something I have to work out.

Of course, there is a considerable difference between a conscious concentration on the patient's situation and an uncalled-for preoccupation or fascination with him. The same holds true if A dreams about P. Something has to be worked on then in his own attitude. He may be unconscious about certain trends in P's psyche or in his own concerning the relationship. Also, if a patient dreams about the analyst one has to consider that the dream may reflect not only the projections of P toward A but also sometimes A's real attitude in the analytic situation. A dream criticizing the analyst must be taken seriously in the sense that A has to ask himself if this criticism tells him something about his own attitude and blind spots. For instance, there is the quite frequent dream that P wants to telephone A, but A is not there or the communication gets cut off. Now A has to ask himself if he is really open enough to P, or what attitude he could take for better communication, or at what point communication breaks off. That the lack of communication is very often the central problem of the *patient* is evident, and one tends to interpret such a dream mainly on the subjective level. But the consideration mentioned first is always very important—namely the question for A of where he stands in the present analytic situation.

All this means that the analytic process really does involve A as well as P. A must be aware of his own power drives, or of his needs to be father or mother, in order to have them under a certain control and to not seek the satisfaction of those needs unconsciously through the analytic relationship. We shall talk about all this (line c) in more detail later.

Now there is one other factor of relationship we have not mentioned so far: the relations between the unconscious of P and the unconscious of A (line b). These are the factors lying in the dark for A, as well as for P. This would be the state of *participation mystique* or identity which Jung has described.[28] It is the area of common unconsciousness between the two partners. I think it is important for any analyst to know that such areas always exist and to watch out for any glimpses he might get into this matter. For instance, both can fall prey to an archetype (that is, identify with it), which they then unconsciously act out together.

Take the archetype of the divine healer. In one form or another we always get infected by the plea of the patient for help, and already the healer archetype may be constellated. We want to give help. We may get overactive in suggesting things which should help the patient to feel better—he should paint, do active imagination, leave the job where he has difficulties, move away from his mother, etc. Things should move, our suggestions should initiate an improvement in the patient's condition—then we can feel ourselves being helpful in a therapeutic way. Sometimes this may even work; often it does not, and disappointment is the result. The analyst may blame the patient for not having the right attitude toward therapy, or he may despair about his own capacities as an analyst. The feeling is that he just does not know how to help this patient.

Now, any Jungian analyst knows that it is not his job to heal. Help can come only through a transformation of the patient's attitude, through his coming into a right relationship with his unconscious. But once the analyst is caught unconsciously by the healer archetype, this knowledge may be used overzealously and with premature timing. The emotional need to help wants an outlet.

In mythology the archetype of the healer is depicted in the image of Asclepius and often also of his father, Apollo. Now, Apollo is associated with the muses, with artistic and spiritual creativity, with the oracle; but he is also the shooter of arrows. His arrows can heal, but they can also wound and kill. The overactivity of an analyst when he is caught in the healer archetype reminds me sometimes of the arrows of Apollo. He has to shoot interpretations, suggestions and advice at the patient to fulfil his own need to help and heal. The result cannot be foreseen. For the patient, it may seem as if his plea for help is met by demands from the analyst—he should do this, and that, in order to feel better. These arrows into his wound *may* do the trick. The energy of the healer archetype can induce him to meet these demands; he may feel some initial results, and a fruitful process may get started. But the demands may, for instance, also touch a difficult father complex which is unconscious. All the patient feels then is his inability to meet the demands and advice of the analyst. This can put him into despair about himself or cause great resistance to the analyst. And there is mutual despair—the patient feels he cannot get help, and the analyst feels he cannot help him. Sometimes there are helpful dreams in such situations, but by no means always, especially if the patient is resisting.

The problem may be that the analyst is unconscious of the impact his therapeutic enthusiasm has on the patient. That is why it is generally important to watch out for how the "demands" of classical Jungian analysis—writing down dreams, keeping a diary, painting, etc.—are experienced by the analysand. But if things get stuck this way, there is still the possibility of realizing their mutual participation in the healer archetype. Frustrations and bad experiences can lead the analyst to some insight as to *why* the patient seems unable to accept and make use of his help. Going into this question with the patient may also reveal his father complex, which was constellated and transferred to the analyst as a result of the analyst's demands. The analysis of childhood material may then become of foremost importance: experiences which are related to the father have been transferred to the analyst and can therefore get analyzed to a certain degree.

All kinds of mutual influences and seductions can take place in an area of mutual unconsciousness. The "mother-child" or "father-child" relationship is very often acted out unconsciously. The analyst's need to mother may induce a dependent childlike attitude in the patient, and vice versa. Often the patient seduces the analyst to be overprotective—to take special care, to worry about the patient's exams, etc.—but it may also be the other way around. In this area there can be a kind of fusion between the unconscious needs and fantasies of analyst and analysand. The patient may have a dream showing the exact psychic situation of the analyst. Or the analyst may have a sudden, "irrational" anxiety attack concerning the patient and contact him by telephone, thereby preventing a suicide attempt. Telepathic and synchronistic events between the two are based also on this constellation.

Does Transference Influence Dreams?

It was Jung's view that dreams are autonomous, spontaneous events which cannot be influenced directly. Freudians are generally of the opinion that transference influences dreams to a high degree—that the wish to please the analyst may produce dreams which the analyst likes or expects and which are in line with his or her views and concepts. In consequence, there would be "Freudian" or "Jungian" dreams, according to the standpoint of the analyst.

As far as I know there is no evidence that dreams are produced just because the analyst likes a special kind of dream. But it is true that through analysis dream contents and dream actions often change. As soon as we are in analysis, the contents of the analytical discussions are also conscious preoccupations to which the unconscious reacts accordingly. It is also a fact that we consciously know the dreams will be discussed with the analyst. We somehow do not dream only for ourselves anymore. This conscious knowledge has an impact on our dream life. Dreams are therefore very often messages to the analyst.

All this seems fairly obvious. Now the question is, whether the unconscious fusion between patient and analyst, referred to above, also influences the content of dreams. I think we cannot deny this possibility. And that would mean that dreams could unconsciously be induced by the analyst. I want to give you an example.

In a psychiatric hospital I treated a twenty-five-year-old woman who suffered from a serious condition due to an extremely negative influence from her mother. She showed all the symptoms which Erich Neumann describes in connection with a disturbed primary relationship between mother and child.[29] Basically she felt that she had no right to live, she did not belong to the human race, everybody despised her, and God did not allow her a better fate than to be punished. Of course she transferred or projected all these contents also onto me, feeling that I despised her, made fun of her and rejected her. She could not bear it when I looked at her, as she felt herself to be terribly ugly, and often she would hardly talk because she felt that everything she said was stupid and that I would reject her even more. To the tenth session she brought the following dream:

> I am in a large room. We are about ten girls waiting for therapy. Dr. Jacoby enters and questions us all to find out who knows anything of the meaning of the name J.S. Bach. A girl says something about Isis and Osiris. Consequently Dr. Jacoby chooses this girl and goes out with her.

Elsewhere I have examined this dream in detail,[30] but in connection with our question of whether the analyst can unconsciously induce dreams of patients, there are some striking facts. The patient had heard in the hospital that I was very interested in music and that I had been a professional musician. She herself was musical to some degree and liked to play the piano. Her whole striving at that time was to be loved and accepted by me, but she had the constant fear of rejection and the belief that God or fate would not allow her to be loved and accepted. She was hardly aware of me as a human partner but had already built me into her complex-world of wanting to be loved but being rejected. Now she dreams about J.S. Bach, about something which concerns me very deeply.

On her side, the dream might reflect an unconscious attempt to get really close to me. Bach is in reality my favourite composer. His music is profoundly religious, and he expressly wrote his works for the glory of God only. His fugues, works of genius constructed in accordance with strict laws, can bring about in a listener the experience of timelessness bound to time, in the same way that the mandala seeks to represent the transcendent through geometric order. Psychologically speaking, Bach's fugues may be seen as symbols of wholeness. There is another most meaningful detail in this connection. In the dream the analyst asks about the meaning of the *name* of J.S. Bach. Now, Bach used the letters of his name, B A C H, as a basic theme for one of his fugues. He died when he was working on this very fugue, based on the theme made out of the letters of his name. (In English: b-flat, a, c, b; in German: B, identical with b-flat, H with b.) His lifework was completed. These are most impressive connections, none of them known to the dreamer.

But further: a girl in the dream answers "something about

Isis and Osiris," and that does seem to be the right answer. The patient's association to Isis and Osiris was Mozart's "Magic Flute." It happens that Mozart, next to Bach, is my favourite composer. His "Magic Flute" is mainly concerned with the overcoming of the power of the dark goddess—the central problem of this patient. Erich Neumann has published an interesting psychological interpretation of the libretto of Mozart's "Magic Flute."[31] As mentioned before, I had viewed this girl's symptomatology and life-history in light of Neumann's work on disturbances of the primary relationship, so Neumann was very much in my mind in connection to her. In the "Magic Flute," the Queen of Night wants to use her daughter Pamina to murder Sarastro, the priest of light, in order to bring the solar circle under her whip. "The vengeance of hell" is boiling in her heart, the subject of her famous aria. But through her daughter Pamina's strong love for the prince Tamino, which first has to hold true in the test of fire and water, the girl is liberated from the power of her vengeful mother and is initiated into the cult of Isis and Osiris.

All this was of course very far from the patient's consciousness. For her, it was only important that in the dream I chose not *her,* but the girl who knew about Isis and Osiris, the one who knew the right answer; this was proof of how I rejected her. But taking the dream on the subjective level, the girl who knew about Isis and Osiris was a part of herself, which in reality was projected onto her sister. Her sister was an artist, and my patient felt that she herself had always been in the shadow of her gifted and beautiful sister, toward whom she had intense feelings of both admiration and envy. But according to the dream, this "sister" was also in her: it was that positive artistic and imaginative part of her which had found contact with me and touched me.

I was truly moved by that dream—somehow it could also have been a dream of my own in connection with that patient. She had dreamed about something which really concerned me, not only in relation to her but also in a general way. As a matter of fact, the dream really belonged to us both, although she was not yet in a position to understand its impact. And how on earth did she come to have such a dream? I can only speculate that it must have been born in our area of mutual unconsciousness. I had not been quite conscious of the extent to which the fate of this girl had already gotten under my skin. Whether it was her dream or mine, it contained a message of very deep meaning, which I could of course grasp better at that moment than she could, and which gave me an inner direction for the analysis.

It seems obvious that this dream would not have happened if this woman had not been in analysis with me. That she had a deep wish to please me and to be accepted is clear also. The astonishing fact is only the extent to which her unconscious grasped my own wavelength in dimensions which were far away from her consciousness. The dream had been *constellated,* as a Jungian would say, by the analytic encounter. And "constellation" means of course that she had this dream not only for the sake of pleasing me. To look at it that way would be a "nothing but" attitude. I had to consider it as referring to aspects of herself which began to be awakened through the relationship with me. As a matter of fact, this dream was an initial dream, and its contents were slowly realized in the course of the analysis.

Transference, Identity and Projection

The preceding section illustrates quite well what can happen due to the unconscious connection between analyst and analysand (line **b** in the diagram on page 25). Unlike a conscious communication between one specific, personal ego and another distinctly separate one (line **a**), the unconscious connection indicates a state of identity or fusion, a oneness of the two.

In analysis this connection is called transference-countertransference, but any strong emotional tie involves this same state of what Jung calls *participation mystique.*[32] The other person is a part of myself and the other way around. The sexual drive, wanting to unite with the other person (becoming "one flesh," as the Bible says), is the concrete physical side of this experience. It illustrates the basic human need to fuse with another person. The moment of orgasm, if fully experienced, brings a loss of ego-control and therefore a temporary loss of identity. Behind symptoms of impotence or frigidity, therefore, there is very often anxiety about giving up ego-control, of losing one's identity to one's partner and being at his or her mercy.

In any essentially healthy relationship, and often in analysis, the feeling-tones associated with this kind of identification are agreeable. But we can readily observe partners with strong emotional ties whose aim seems to be to destroy each other. This is popularly known as a "love-hate relationship." Edward Albee in his play "Who's Afraid of Virginia Woolf?" gives a startling portrayal of this kind of tie.

I know of one marriage, for instance, in which the destiny of each partner seems to be to inflict psychic torture on the other. Any objective outsider with sound reasoning would say that divorce would be the only way out. But if the husband leaves for a business trip of even two days—which happens not too often—he telephones his wife and complains of loneliness without her. He does not know how to spend an evening on his own. At one point the wife complained that she could not live with this man any more—if only she could have a few days' somewhere away from him! The opportunity for a vacation in the southern part of Switzerland came. She was with good friends—but the next morning she was lying in bed crying because her husband was not there and she missed him so much.

There also exist destructive friendships between persons of the same sex or business relationships of a competitive kind involving strong emotional ties between people who hate each other. The partners actually seem to need each other in order to act out their aggressive and destructive impulses.

It is because of all these complications that human relationships are so difficult. Working at a relationship problem consists of trying to become conscious of one's own part in the game. From the point of view of ego-consciousness, these complications are projections of what is going on down below. This means that as soon as the first glimpse of awareness, or a slight feeling of unreality, enters the mind of one of the partners, the state of complete *identity* begins to break down and it becomes possible to differentiate the *projection* of certain unconscious contents.[33] This often first takes the form of disappointment in the behavior of the partner: he or she does not behave, act, or feel as we thought.

For instance, a young couple may be very much in love. They are one soul and one body and everything is just wonderful: for them it is an experience of heaven. Now if you come and say, "You feel that way only because you project an unconscious side of yourself," you psychologize the relationship in a destructive way. Why should these young people not have the important experience of paradise through fusion? The couple would either be angry at you or would laugh at your psychological explanations and decide that you don't have the slightest clue about what real love means—and rightly so.

Unfortunately, sooner or later the honeymoon comes to an end. One partner starts to suffer because the other does not fulfil certain expectations, and problems arise. *Now* it might be possible to talk about expectations and show which of these have to do with a projected animus or anima image— and only now can we properly talk of projection. The process of taking back the projections enlarges consciousness and results in a state of individual separateness. The two partners may then relate on a different level, recognizing and accepting the other's individual strengths and weaknesses.

The Therapeutic Value of Countertransference

Jung's view that analysis is a dialectical process in which doctor and patient are involved as whole persons,[34] brings the so-called countertransference of the analyst into focus. Freud, already in 1910, first recognized some of the importance of the countertransference.[35] He saw it mainly as a danger for the analyst to lose the neutrality which he considered essential to making correct interpretations of the patient's unconscious conflicts. Countertransference feelings were to be avoided as much as possible and eliminated by analysis or at least self-analysis. Jung was not of the same opinion. He felt that the analyst cannot help becoming at times even deeply affected by his patient, and that he had better accept this fact and be as conscious of it as possible.

It was not until 1950 that a number of papers appeared by Freudian psychoanalysts showing that countertransference is not only an obstacle in the analytic treatment but may also be used to uncover unconscious dynamics going on in the patient.[36] For instance, Heinrich Racker's book *Transference and Countertransference* (1968), containing papers written by him mainly during the 1950s, gives detailed accounts of interactional dynamics between transference and countertransference. One is reminded of Jung's model of the dialectical interrelation between two partners when Racker emphasizes that in the analytic situation two persons are involved—each with a neurotic part and a healthy part, a past and a present, and a relation to fantasy and reality. Each is both an adult and a child, having feelings toward each other of a child to a parent and a parent to a child.[37]

Thus the analysand can also be experienced unconsciously by the analyst as a parental figure. If the analyst is open enough to watch his feeling-reactions before the patient comes or in the course of the sessions, he may for instance find himself anxious not to disappoint the expectations of the patient. Or he may with a certain patient feel rather stupid and unable to come up with a meaningful insight at all. Another analysand may constellate in him impulses to share some of his own problems because that analysand seems so warm, mature and understanding.

These are just examples of what may occur, feelings which if consciously reflected upon might be seen as signs of a somewhat unrealistic response from the analyst's side. Is that patient really so demanding and oversensitive that the fear of disappointing his expectations is realistic? Or is this reaction partly or entirely based on a counterprojection of a parental figure within the analyst, for instance a love-demanding mother who was narcissistically hurt by the slightest move of independent self-assertion? In this case the analyst unconsciously experiences his patient as if he had expectations like his mother's; he is afraid of loss of love if he disappoints his patient.

Or say he is unable to come up with a meaningful interpretation, and then begins to feel inadequate—could this mean that his patient is resisting, and identifying in a defensive way with his grandiosity, which has the effect of making the analyst feel stupid? Or does the analyst project onto the patient an overcritical parental figure for whom nothing was ever good enough? Both interpretations can of course be true, and as mentioned before it is of tremendous importance to be open to the constant possibility of falling into what the Freudian psychoanalyst Racker calls *neurotic countertransference* — which the Jungian Michael Fordham calls *illusory countertransference*.[38] If such projections are not recognized, they can be damaging to the analytic process and do harm to the patient.

Yet analysts now realize that countertransference can as well be used for the benefit of the analysis, since it is also an interaction with the transference of the patient. This is called *syntonic countertransference* by Fordham, in contrast to the illusory countertransference.[39] Racker has proposed the term *countertransference proper* in distinction to neurotic countertransference. He differentiates countertransference proper (Fordham's syntonic type) into two forms, namely the *concordant countertransference* and the *complementary countertransference*.[40] I feel this is a useful distinction and want to give examples for each.

Recently a woman training to be an analyst came for supervision and brought with her for the first time a tape of an analytic session she had had with a woman patient of hers. To our amazement, in listening to this tape, we both had at certain times quite some difficulty in distinguishing her own voice from the voice of the patient. This happened mostly when the patient was talking very softly and obviously fighting to overcome feelings of shame. The candidate felt rather shocked at first and asked me whether she might be identified with the patient in an unhealthy way. I heard her interventions on the tape as being genuinely in tune to the atmosphere and situation of the patient at those moments, so I told her that to my mind she was responding in an empathic way to her patient. It was apparent that the patient needed this kind of response, for later on the tape one could hear that the patient became more confident in exploring her own feelings. I think that this candidate reacted to the needs of her patient with a *concordant* countertransference reaction.

I am probably experiencing concordant countertransference when I can allow myself to be spontaneously with the patient wherever he really needs me to be, and when I can be open and flexible enough to allow him to "use" me to a wide extent, according to his needs within the symbolic framework of the therapeutic situation. It is of course important for the analyst to be at the same time as aware as possible of where this is leading. But I have seen again and again that if I can let myself be "carried" to where the patient vitally seems to need me, I experience a deep sense of empathy which allows sensitive new insights to appear spontaneously.

Quite often feelings, emotions, thoughts or intuitions pop up in me which are in the patient's mind and which he may express at that very moment. I am always amazed at these synchronistic or "quasi-telepathic" incidents. It is then a question of whether to mention this simultaneous experience or not. If I tell the patient that I was thinking just then exactly what he said, he may experience this as being too intrusive or may become afraid of not being able to keep secrets from me, since I am obviously able to "see through" him. Thus there may be a fear of his ego-boundaries being invaded. However, I have often found it to be valuable to share this common ground with the analysand. It may satisfy in a therapeutically important way his deep longing to be truly understood and empathized with. He may also begin to have more trust in the manifestations of the unconscious. Concordant countertransference therefore has a lot to do with the analyst getting in touch with the patient and with experiencing what Jung has called mystical participation.

Now let us consider a different incident. A young woman, an analysand of mine for over a year, came one day to the session and said, "I just don't know whether I dreamt this or whether it really happened." She uttered this statement in a somewhat withdrawn, depressive and slightly childlike tone of voice. I heard myself reply rather quickly and with a slightly harsh and irritated tone: "Surely you *must know* whether something is a dream or reality." After this there was silence on both sides.

As we sat there, I realized that my quick reaction had come from a sudden shocklike fear that this patient might become psychotic, as she apparently no longer knew the boundaries between reality and dream; then I had felt an immediate reaction to deny this suspicion: It just cannot be true, I have to tell her positively that she *does* know, she *must* know the boundaries.

We both continued sitting there in silence. I felt astonished at my reaction, which was quite foreign to my usual way of responding to patients in general and to this analysand in particular. "What strange and inadequate behavior," I heard a voice say in myself. And with this an idea popped up: that I had behaved like a parent who is worried when the child is not behaving reasonably and fears that something might be wrong with him. The parent's defence is immediate denial: It just cannot be true, I do not want it to be true. This idea seemed to be consistent with a growing insight into what was happening between us and thus gave me some relief.

I observed my analysand sitting there silently in a sulky mood. And just as I was wondering how I might bring up my understanding of what was happening between us, she said: "You know, I just felt very angry at you. You behaved exactly like my mother." So there it was. I told her that I had just come up with the same realization and that I had asked myself why I behaved in such a strange way. I added that I might have made a mistake by reacting in such a way but that at least I knew now very well how her mother must have behaved and what effect this behavior must have had on her, my analysand.

Now the ground was prepared to get into the question of what in my patient might have prompted my behavior, and whether and under what circumstances she *provokes* people in her surroundings to behave toward her as her mother did. In my patient's view her mother had been overanxious about the child's well-being, yet when the child had a real complaint she denied it, saying that it could not be so. These reactions had made my patient feel stupid, not taken seriously, even unreal. Mother always "knew" that the things the child experienced were not true experiences, thus my patient was still somewhat confused as to whether her own experiences could be felt as real and valuable or whether she should listen to her constant doubts about them. This confusion used to lead her into regressive attitudes where "mother knows best," and I think that it was such a regression that she unconsciously enacted with me.

With this woman I obviously acted out countertransference

impulses of the kind Racker calls *complementary.* I virtually became the patient's mother, the most important figure of her past, an image or complex which was still operating within her at present. Strictly speaking, it was a mistake for me to incorporate and enact that figure so unconsciously—I had fallen into a trap laid unconsciously by my patient. Would it not have been better to simply dispassionately interpret what was going on between us? Yet the power of the complex thus became very vivid for both of us, and from a deeper viewpoint my mistake may even have been necessary. Anyway, it did no harm once it was recognized—on the contrary, for I had not previously been in empathy with the feelings of my patient; if I had, I might have commented on how her confusion must feel and what it might mean. Her regressive tone of voice had constellated in me a resistance against responding from a concordant point of view, which would have been more "correct"; instead, my response arose from a complementary countertransference.

Earlier I gave some brief examples of so-called neurotic or illusory countertransference, where the analyst feels rather stupid or blocked, and unable to arrive at any meaningful insight. In such a case, is he projecting onto the patient an overcritical parental figure for whom nothing was ever good enough? This really would be a sign of illusory countertransference. But I also mentioned the possibility that the patient is defensively identifying with his grandiosity (inflation) and in his "omniscience" knows everything better. Then the analyst's feeling might be a response to the inner state of the patient. In that case it would be a complementary countertransference response.

Naturally it can happen that the analyst has such an inflated, omniscient parental figure in himself, which at the slightest opportunity can make him feel stupid and inadequate, and which of course gets projected wherever there is a hook. And the hook is usually a patient with a similar problem. Thus it is often very difficult to make out whether the analyst is experiencing illusory or complementary countertransference. Is he projecting upon the patient or is he perceiving something in the patient via his countertransference feelings? Is it projection or perception?

In the example I gave of myself enacting my patient's mother, it was not too difficult to see the complementarity of the countertransference. I behaved in an unusual way. But often one's reactions do not feel so strange, but have only an increased emotional intensity. I think the reason why it is so important to be in touch with one's own wounds as much as possible is in order not to do harm to the patient by acting out neurotic transference-countertransference games. Very often countertransference feelings are in fact a mixture of illusory and syntonic, both unconscious projection and genuine perception. The analyst has to be constantly aware of both possibilities and needs to differentiate one from the other to the best of his ability. Thus, the analyst, simply by virtue of his or her daily occupation, is also constantly in analysis—as Jung so clearly points out:

> The patient, by bringing an activated unconscious content to bear upon the doctor, constellates the corresponding unconscious material in him.... [Therefore] contents are often activated in the doctor which might normally remain latent....
>
> Even the most experienced psychotherapist will discover again and again that he is caught up in a bond, a combination resting on mutual unconsciousness. And though he may believe himself to be in possession of all the necessary knowledge concerning the constellated archetypes, he will in the end come to realize that there are very many things indeed of which his academic knowledge never dreamed.[41]

3

Narcissism and Transference

During the last few years there has been much talk about the increase of patients suffering from so-called narcissistic personality disorders. This is a relatively vague diagnosis which may cover a range from very damaged people with pathological narcissism,[42] to nearly all of us, who are apt to suffer in some area from some kind of inferiority complex and its overcompensation. I would have difficulty in naming people who, to a greater or lesser degree, are not vulnerable to narcissistic fluctuations, who are so stable in their sense of self-esteem that they never fall into an unrealistic inflation or are never gripped by feelings of total unworthiness.

Heinz Kohut has written two illuminating books on the subject of narcissistic personality disorders and their psychoanalytic treatment: *The Analysis of the Self* and *The Restoration of the Self*. They show a new approach which deviates somewhat from classical psychoanalysis and is in many ways astonishingly close to certain aspects of Jung's analytical psychology.[43] Kohut points out two main forms of transference he has encountered when dealing with narcissistic personality disorders: the mirror transference and the idealizing transference. I find his observations very useful and in a great many instances much to the point. As Kohut has become quite popular I want to talk briefly about these types of transference from my own Jungian perspective.

The Mirror Transference

The mirror transference, according to Kohut, arises from a basic and vital human need for "empathic resonance."[44] We all need mirroring in order to recognize ourselves, and we need empathic resonance in order to feel real, accepted and therefore valuable to others and in turn valuable to ourselves.

I think in this connection of a Greek myth which is narrated in a hymn of Pindar: When Zeus had put all things in their right order, he celebrated his wedding and asked the Olympian deities whether they thought his creation was complete or whether they still missed and needed something. The gods asked him to create some divine beings who would praise his great deeds and his universe and who would embellish it by words and music. This was the origin of the Muses.[45]

It seems thus that the gods are not satisfied that the universe and life simply exist. The Muses had to be created to give *resonance* to this existence by music, and *re-flection* of it by words. The Muses have the task of praising the deeds of Zeus and of bringing what exists to conscious attention through their music and their words. If this holds true of the macrocosm, how much more does a microcosm, the fragile and vulnerable individual human being, need praise, resonance and mirroring of his existence?

If nobody in the whole world is taking joy in the fact that I exist, if there is nobody who understands, appreciates and loves what I am and what I do, then there is hardly any chance of keeping a healthy narcissistic balance, a realistic sense of self-esteem. Such a basic sense of isolation is often at the bottom of the suffering symptomatic of the extreme narcissistic personality disorder. Nobody is "there" to give mirroring and empathic resonance. This may actually be true in reality, but usually it has to do with an inner psychic difficulty: nobody can be trusted to come near enough to perform these vitally needed functions.

This lack of basic trust is usually a sign of damage in early infancy. With good reason one has to stress the fact that the first and most decisive mirror of the existence of any human being is the person who takes care of the infant after its birth. The infant has not yet a sense of identity independent of the mother; mother and child form a symbiotic unity.[46] The mother is experienced by the infant as part of itself, and therefore Kohut coined the paradoxical term "self-object." In any case, development of a realistic and relatively stable sense of self-esteem in later life depends to a large degree on the empathic resonance and sensitive mirroring a mother is able to give to her child. "The gleam in the mother's eye" is a phrase used by Kohut to describe this first mirror when it is

reflecting joy in the baby's existence and its various activities.

Patients who form a mirror transference have usually had some distorted mirroring in the past and therefore have difficulties in knowing who they are and in feeling welcome on this earth in a realistic enough way. They have developed oversensitive "feelers" which pick up the slightest sign of possible rejection, with a traumatizing effect on their sense of self. One defence against this constant threat is the development of an overcompensatory conviction: I do not need anybody at all, I can be completely self-sufficient. This is in fact an unconscious identification with infantile feelings of omnipotence —with the "grandiose self," to use Kohut's terminology.

Of course people with this psychic constellation come in to analysis only if the overcompensatory defence system gets shaken. First of all, then, their sense of self-importance has to be restored; they thus form a mirror transference in the sense that the analyst has no right to an autonomous existence of his own, but is reduced to functioning as a mirror to reflect their grandiosity, specialness and self-sufficiency. The countertransference response of the analyst is often to feel devalued, useless and impotent.

According to differing theories about the psychodynamics

behind the grandiose self, the two most important pioneers in the field of narcissism, Heinz Kohut and Otto Kernberg, give differing techniques for handling it. Kohut is of the opinion that the grandiose self constitutes a fixation at the level of the infantile illusions of omnipotence and omniscience, to which the patient has regressed. He therefore needs empathic resonance from the analyst, sometimes for quite a long period, which may enable him to gradually develop a more realistic sense of self-esteem.[47] This procedure is a kind of corrective emotional response from the analyst. Kernberg sees the grandiose self with its tendency to devalue the analyst mainly as a compensatory defence against a flood of archaic envy. He therefore pleads for interpretation of the defences in order to show the patient what he is doing with the analyst.[48] He is thus using countertransference responses of the complementary type as a source for interpretation.

In practice either response may at times be adequate—or sometimes inadequate. In many instances I very much feel that "empathic resonance" or "holding" (in the sense used by D.W. Winnicott)[49] is the attitude most urgently needed by the patient. Even if my function as an analyst seems completely unimportant and useless, the direct or more often indirect reproaches about my uselessness will increase as soon as the patient feels a lack of empathic response from me. He thus has to admit, if indirectly, my significance for him, in addition to the fact that he continues to come.

Yet for me this mirroring and holding function often conflicts with my conviction that the patient really needs true and genuine responses. He has to rely on the fact that the mirroring he may get from the analyst does not again distort his self-image. Whenever I get impulses to change my attitude, however, I have to ask myself first whether I may be feeling personally hurt about the "uselessness" to which I am reduced. Am I personally also frustrated because I am not allowed to get near any of the true yet oversensitive feelings of the patient? Of course these feelings of hurt and frustration may be legitimate human responses to the way I am treated. But the main question for the analysis is always whether I can sense not only personal hurt, but also signs indicating empathy with the patient and therefore syntonic countertransference. My impulses may be composed of a mixture of the two, yet if syntonic countertransference reactions are in the foreground, I can give the patient some hints about his defences as I see them and about his way of treating me—and probably anybody else who comes near enough. That would be an interpretation out of complementary countertransference feelings.

I am reminded in this connection of a young man full of so-called narcissistic rage. An enormous anger would flare up whenever he felt that his brilliant talents as an artist were not recognized by others. He was full of bitter envy of those who had "made it," although in his opinion they were much less talented than he was, and were successful only because of their money or their influential parents. All this was proof to him of the injustice of our society, against which he was full of spite. He used me as a sounding board for his aggression and watched me carefully with the urgent expectation that I agree with everything he said. It became more and more difficult during this phase of his analysis to question the slightest of his utterances, and for several weeks I had resigned myself to the role of passive listener to his tirades, thinking that it might be valuable for him finally to be able to express his aggression openly. But at the same time I felt bored stiff and somehow alienated from him. His aggressive behavior also created some difficulties for his career in the outside world, which caused him astonishment. He wanted to be loved for his hate.

One day he came with the following dream: He was in a desert like the Sahara. Suddenly the sand became soft and he sank into it deeper and deeper until finally even his head was covered with sand and only both arms were still outstretched, waving for help. From this he woke up in intense fear.

In response to this dream I experienced an immediate impulse to take these hands, so to speak, and try to pull him out of that engulfing sand. I felt that now I needed to "handle" his problem quite actively. Since he was very frightened about the dream, he could finally give me a chance to be heard. So I was able to show him how he was sinking deeper and deeper into his illusions about life and about his extraordinary talents, getting "sand in his eyes" to a dangerous degree. I also told him how I had felt manipulated into the role of powerless listener. Of course I added that I could empathize and understand these defences, which may have been necessary for his survival from his difficult childhood on. Yet now, as the dream shows, they obviously had become very destructive. I told him my conviction that if he could let go of the illusions which were triggering so much rage in him, he would find in himself genuine talents and real values. I especially mentioned in detail some of the potential which I truly felt he had.

He left this session completely shattered and came back the next time saying that he had very much doubted whether he would come to see me again, but had found after a while that it had been the most decisive session. He then asked me why I had not told him earlier how I really felt about him. We could then again discuss his defences against any intervention from my side. And finally, we both had some feelings of gratitude toward his own unconscious resources which had provided that dream as a crystallizing point for a change in our attitudes.

Thus we find at one end of a scale a form of mirror transference which needs to devalue the analyst. At the other end of the same scale, I have often experienced patients with a form of mirror transference in which the analyst is experienced as indispensable for their inner balance. He is very much overvalued and the slightest of his responses determines whether the patient feels okay or whether he doubts his right to exist at all. Every word and tone of voice, every minute gesture, can be experienced by the patient as indicating acceptance or rejection, as if it were a verdict of the mirror. The way these patients use the analyst often reminds me of the queen in Grimm's fairytale "Snow-White" who anxiously had to enquire, "Mirror, mirror, on the wall, who is the fairest one of all?" If the mirror did not give the reassurance that she was indeed "the fairest one of all," the queen was shocked and got "green and yellow with envy." Similarly, if a patient suffering from narcissistic wounds doubts the analyst's mirroring of his (or her) unique specialness, he may be flooded with feelings of envy and jealousy. In his or her fantasy all the other patients are then surely much more interesting, intelligent and beautiful.

In the beginning of an analysis those mirroring expectations are often repressed and hidden from consciousness, and it is important to allow space for them to come into the open. Since the analyst in his mirroring function is unconsciously experienced as part of the patient's own self (Kohut's "self-object"), it is natural that a patient suffers from attacks of possessiveness once he realizes that the analyst is also mirroring many other people who might even be preferred to himself. This feels like the loss of a part of himself. For the analyst it is important to be able to empathize with these deeply rooted fears, in order not to feel imprisoned by the bothersome attacks of possessiveness. Otherwise he may have angry impulses to free himself from these "prison chains" by rude, aggressive or mocking remarks. Such rejection is naturally detrimental to the analysis.

As said before, there are patients who need constant "empathic resonance" to the slightest of their utterances for long phases of their analysis. Yet I myself have made it more or less a rule in my therapeutic work not to venture an interpretation or a response before experiencing in myself a "gut reaction" to what the patient has said. Otherwise there is the danger of making empty, routine interventions. But this can sometimes cause difficulties in cases of mirror transference.

I remember for instance a patient who was talking about a rather delicate subject and I simply could not find at once a response or interpretation which seemed genuinely adequate to my feelings. So I sat there silently, letting what he had said sink into me and awaiting what would come up, yet at the same time troubled by my growing awareness that some kind of response from me was needed then and there. If he dared to approach such a delicate subject I couldn't just let him be without "empathic resonance," or else his feelings of shame would make him withdraw into his shell again. Yet nothing came up in me. It helped the situation that we had by that time fairly adequately worked through his fears of provoking my rejection whenever he made critical remarks. He was therefore now able to remark shyly that he suddenly felt as if he were talking against a wall. To this I could reply that his feeling matched my own discomfort at not having an adequate response at hand in spite of being aware that it was urgently needed. I told him that I had to let what he said sink in before being able to give a genuine response. At this, he felt once again understood and taken seriously. At the same time he also had to acknowledge a bit of my personal autonomy, which is an important step in the gradual transformation of mirror transference.

The goal of this hoped-for transformation process is, in general, a decrease of dependence on outside mirroring through an increased sense of realistic self-esteem, and thus also a greater sense of personal autonomy.

The Idealizing Transference

What Heinz Kohut terms idealizing transference is, in Jungian terminology, to a large degree similar to the projection of archetypal images upon the analyst. According to Kohut, this form of transference is based on the repetition of the fact that the infant needs for the development of its self not only empathic mirroring of its existence and sense of omnipotence, but also experiences of the parents as all-powerful, omniscient and perfect. But since in this very early phase of development the parental figure is hardly distinguishable from the infant's own self—therefore called a self-object—the perfection of the admired figure means also its own perfection. One could say that a fusion with the omnipotence of the parental figure takes place. It is the gradual disappointment upon finding that the parental figure is in many respects not as omniscient, all-powerful and perfect as expected, which later on helps the child mature into an independent adult.

In other words, self-esteem can also develop and be sustained when, out of fusion with the idealized self-object, ideals have been born that stimulate worthwhile transpersonal commitment. The same holds true with idealizing transference: in optimal analytical development the patient will gradually suffer disappointment due to the analyst's limitations, and this will lead to his "transmuting internalisation."[50] It is important that the analyst be able to tolerate being an idealized figure as long as this is needed by the patient, because abrupt disappointments can have a traumatizing effect and be detrimental to the analytic process.

The idealizing capacity, then, is already operative in infancy and remains potentially active throughout life. It is surely connected if not equivalent to what Jungians call creative archetypal fantasy. Omnipotence, for instance, is an archetypal quality which in general is attributed to a godhead. Idealizing transference is therefore in my opinion, as already mentioned, a projection of an archetypal content upon the analyst. The gradual disappointment in the analyst is part of the general process of "taking back projections." This means discovering the formerly projected contents in one's own psyche—a process of becoming conscious of something about oneself which because of its unconsciousness had been experienced as a characteristic of someone else.

To give an example, I remember a young man suffering from a severe form of agoraphobia and many unspecific psychosomatic complaints. In the beginning he did not allow me to "be there" as a human person who was trying to alleviate his complaints by possible helpful interventions. Yet, in contrast to the patient mentioned before, he did not give me the feeling that I was useless to him. On the contrary, I rather felt that he experienced me in a threatening way as incredibly strong and omnipotent. He swamped me with constant talk so that I could not get a word in, and whenever I tried to open my mouth I observed a defensive gesture with his hands. One day, seemingly out of the blue, he was able to gather courage and shout at me: "Whatever you are going to do to me, one thing I will never allow you—to take away my belief in God!" He had been a member of a religious brotherhood. When he fell ill, the brothers had accused him of not believing in Christ in the right way. And when he wanted to consult a psychotherapist, he was scolded and told that only Christ can heal and that all psychotherapists are just worldly sinners. Yet the "worldly sinner" was tremendously attractive for him as well as deathly frightening. The patient had to take leave of the brotherhood and in his desperation consulted me—though with a guilty conscience.

It soon became clear that in his fantasy I had already grown from a worldly sinner into the Antichrist in person, so to speak. I constellated for him the temptation of hell, which was terrifying and fascinating at the same time. Yet he was very much afraid of the verdict in the coming "last judgment" — his form of archaic superego-religion — if he should give in to his strong need to become a part of my world. He saw me as the embodiment of his own instinctive, sexual and aggressive aspects. I was for him the living archetype of the shadow, which had become so black, evil and frightful because it had not been allowed to "incarnate" in himself, it had not been tolerated as a part of him from the very beginning of his life. He had been an unwanted child and had from early on nursed the illusional fantasy that his existence could be accepted and welcomed only if he were "good" in a humanly impossible way. But since indeed he had never been able to be so "good," there had never been any chance of getting accepted.

During the course of the analysis his gradual disappointments in me — I wasn't nearly as evil as he at first imagined — were partly welcomed by him. As he slowly discovered that I was not pure evil, that I was not going to lure him into sin and eternal damnation, taking back some of these projections went hand in hand with a little more tolerance toward his own sexual fantasies and actions. He began to allow himself some critical thoughts about his parents and about the religiosity of his brotherhood, even though critical thought might be evil doubts. I became somewhat more "humanized," and he began to accept the "evil" tendencies in himself as being part of any human being.

This example shows an idealization with a negative or at least ambivalent feeling-tone, in which I was experienced as a demonic figure. I especially wanted to mention this form of idealizing transference, for in general one understands by idealization the projection of an archetypal content which is experienced by the analysand as highly valuable. It can go so far that the analyst seems to embody all the value of what Jung called the Self.

I remember, in the beginning of my training at the Jung Institute in Zurich, meeting an elderly lady who had just come from a session with Jung himself. When she told me this, I felt a mixture of envy, awe and curiosity, as I at that time had never seen him. I asked her: "How is Jung really?" "Oh, you know," she said, with a tone of adoration, "he is like God." I was taken aback, disappointed that she could not give a more differentiated description. I also asked myself whether this woman might be slightly psychotic to think that Jung was God. But then I rightly reminded myself that she had not said Jung *was* God, but that he was *like* Him. She experienced him "as if" he were God and thus had formed what today one could call an idealizing transference. Outstanding individuals such as Jung or Freud are of course attractive "hooks" for the projection of the Self, since the idealization is based on a certain reality and shared by a great number of people.

Both the idealizing transference and the mirror transference occur to some degree in many analyses. Often there is a movement back and forth from one to the other, but they may also appear almost simultaneously.

During three consecutive sessions with one analysand, a woman of about forty, I felt so tired that I had to fight off sleep. The "ideal analyst" in me did not like this at all, but the fact that it happened three times made me realize that it was probably a syntonic countertransference reaction. But what did it mean? The problem could not have been what my patient was talking about, for the subjects were interesting enough even though they were presented in a bit too much detail.

At the time, the woman had been in analysis with me for four years. She had come because of a symptom that was extremely embarrassing for her: she could not pick up a glass of wine, a cup of coffee or a spoon in the presence of other people without her whole arm starting to tremble. This made her feel terribly exposed and flooded with shame, so that she tended more and more to avoid being with people.

And yet my patient had a great gift for listening to and understanding others; her empathy was very well developed. This gift must have been furthered by the fact that from her earliest childhood she had been forced to develop an extreme sensitivity in order to adapt to her mother's constant expectations; it was the only way she could get at least a minimum of vitally needed attention from this obviously narcissistically disturbed woman. Later on in life she continued to give other people's needs priority over her own; whenever she could not fulfil someone's expectations, she was tormented by intense guilt feelings.

In analysis, too, she tried to adapt to my "expectations,"

and she tremendously idealized my "spiritual" side. For her, this idealization meant having to provide me with important dreams and interesting subject matter. Whenever she failed to do so, she felt frightened, ashamed and inferior, and had a sense of inner emptiness. At such moments it was clear that fusion with the idealized self-object—that is, with the highly prized "spiritual principle"—had failed once again. On the whole, my patient showed a lively interest in the analysis, cooperated well, was intelligent and had a highly differentiated feeling for psychological connections. Since she was such a tactful person, her admiration for me did not feel too obtrusive. The stress laid on the spiritual was not too obviously a mere defence against the erotic component, but seemed to correspond to a genuine need in her. And so, in the countertransference thus far, I had generally felt animated by her presence and full of ideas for possible interpretations. Occasionally I found myself delivering lengthy, very knowledgeable explanations, but my analysand seemed to feel nourished and enriched by such discussions, although she sometimes feared that on her way home she would forget all the interesting things she had learned.

As far as her symptoms were concerned, with time there was definite improvement. But we were both aware of the fact that her continuing tendency to feel easily hurt and embarrassed still prevented her from being really spontaneous. However, at this stage of the analysis she no longer hesitated to expose herself to a large group and even to her superiors whenever she felt she had to stand up and fight for an important cause. At such times she had the feeling she was borne up by some transpersonal, spiritual idea—probably a sign of fusion with an idealized self-object. But going to a restaurant and drinking a cup of coffee with the same people still cost her tremendous efforts in trying to overcome her fears of exposure.

I could not shake off her idealizing transference and interpret it as "mere compensation"; it was too vital a matter for her. As mentioned before, the analysand's disappointment that the analyst does not correspond to the ideal fantasy figure has to occur gradually, together with a growing capacity to recognize the projected content as one's own. Thus it can be partially integrated. My analysand also began to express at times some criticism of me, and from the standpoint of the therapy I welcomed this new courage.

But what did my repeated attacks of sleepiness mean? The third time this occurred, I decided not to fight it off, but to discuss it in some way with my analysand. Considering her vulnerability, I felt I could not state the problem directly and tell her she evidently bored me to the point of sleep. What I did was to ask her if at that moment she might have the feeling that she was far away, or even isolated from me. And in fact she was then able to say that she had the impression she was blabbing about completely uninteresting things in which she could naturally not expect *me* to be interested, and thus felt more and more unsure of herself. What she meant, in other words, was that when she did not have my empathic resonance she felt rejected and worthless.

Further analysis of our situation showed that she found herself constantly having to fend off an ever-increasing need: a deep yearning for a mirroring self-object. This need had been deeply buried and was now slowly coming to light. It was a need to be seen and admired, that is, to experience "the gleam in the mother's eye." However, since it was connected with early traumatic memories of disappointment, it was coupled with fear and had to be repressed. All she could consciously experience at this stage of the analysis was intensified fears of not coming up to my expectations and therefore boring me. As my sleepiness indicated, she did manage to bore me and thus to turn me into the unempathic, rejecting maternal figure; at the same time she was unable to communicate to me her real need for a mirroring self-object.

Our efforts at interpreting the emerging mirror transference helped her to express herself more freely whenever she felt that I had misunderstood, hurt or rejected her. This was the beginning of further progress on the way toward self-assertion.

Illusional and Delusional Transference

A few words need to be said about the important distinction between *illusional* and *delusional* transference.[51] As an example, recall the lady I mentioned who apparently experienced Jung like God.

Now, if she had thought that Jung really *was* God, this

would have been a sign of delusional transference. But she said that he was *like* God and thus seemed able to grasp the "as if" or symbolic quality of her experience. Her transference therefore has to be seen as illusional. The young man who experienced me as the Antichrist in person showed signs of delusional transference at the beginning of our encounter. But fairly soon he could talk with me in his better moments about *his fears* that I might be a sort of evil power. This was a sign that he did not entirely believe that I *was* the Antichrist and even trusted me enough to share these fears with me. Thus a working alliance could be formed; I was expected to help him deal with these fears, which showed that the transference was becoming illusional.

The illusional form of transference shows itself by a certain amount of flexibility. It leaves room for being questioned, interpreted and eventually transformed. In essence a patient with an illusional transference could say to his analyst: "I feel sometimes quite strongly and intensely *as if* you were father or mother, lover, teacher, devil or even God. I feel as if you embodied everything I ever wished for or everything I just hate. I feel as if you knew everything, and as if your wonderful perfection has an awfully castrating effect upon me. But somewhere I also know that these feelings have not only to do with you. We might therefore work out together where they come from and where they really belong."

Pure delusions are found of course in psychosis and have to do with a loss of reality. But there is a sliding scale between illusional and delusional transference experiences. In any analysis, episodes of delusional transference may pop up. They often create difficulties since the patient at times may not be able to distance himself from the delusional aspects of his experience. Sometimes they appear in a quite subtle form. A patient might, for instance, experience me as somebody who lures him away from the path of his true self, from his own convictions, like the Pied Piper of Hamlin attracting him and compelling him to be my follower. My kindness is only part of a scheme to form him according to my wishes, to imprison him in my theoretical assumptions, to make him think my thoughts, and so on.

Such arguments do not necessarily appear to be delusional

—rather, they are well-known reproaches which have been directed against psychoanalysis from the very beginning, and in popular opinion the analyst is still often considered to be a brainwashing agent. The suspicions of my patient might even have some truth, and it is important to take this into consideration. One thing is clear, however: the patient is in a state of resistance. And for the time being this must in any case be respected. I cannot *prove* to him that I am in no way a Pied Piper. (Can I ever prove to myself that I have no tendencies whatsoever in this direction?) Yet I might become convinced that my patient's defences against influences from very intrusive and unempathic parents were from early on a matter of psychic survival. He had to use an enormous amount of energy to find and hold to his own path. His still active defences against all kinds of influences and intrusions are therefore understandable. Thus it seems fairly obvious that his anxious fantasies about me consist of projections of powerful, inner parental figures who are attacking his autonomy.

But if I try to interpret these connections to him he feels that I just want to influence him with all that analytical stuff he should believe in. He says that it is exactly my sadistic analytical knife which always cuts him off from his own path toward self-realization. He interprets his dreams the way he needs to see them and I am supposed to agree. Anything I might bring up or question in connection with his dreams is again turned around and feeds the delusion that I want to lure him away from his true path. Still, he is not psychotic and he also continues to come to analysis because he "likes me as a person." Also, there is suffering, and "we still have a lot to work out," he might say.

The delusions in such cases thus affect only part of the personality. For the analyst it is a time to be patient with these defences and sensitive to the slightest signs of an eventually growing trust. After all, it is a fundamental distrust which nourishes the delusional experience. Only growing trust might allow the patient to risk considering the possibility that I might actually not be an intruder into his integrity, but that he is compelled by some inner force to experience me *as if* I were one. Such an insight would be the basis for further analysis of the dynamics behind these fears. Once the illusional transference is more in the foreground, the patient is also able to tell me more specifically at what point he experiences me as intrusive or directive, and thus the mutual interactions become more flexible and vivid. He does not need his global defence anymore. Sometimes he might even realize that he has to defend "his own" against inner attacking doubts so strongly that his sense of identity itself has become very rigid.

Yet in general we have to say that analysis can be very difficult and can become stuck if transference delusions remain resistant. Here we get into the wide field of psychotherapy with psychotic patients, and the average analyst is wise to acknowledge his limitations and leave these cases to the specialist.

Mirror transference, idealizing transference and archetypal transference are terms designating the unconscious expectations a patient is having of his analyst. They have to do with the way in which a patient unconsciously needs to use his analyst. The terms illusional and delusional in reference to transference try to indicate the degree to which the analyst, in spite of the transference, can simultaneously also be perceived as a real person. Every transference is at least illusional. The analyst is seen not only as his real self but also *as if* he were, for example, omniscient. The more delusion in the transference, the less the analyst *can also* be experienced as the real Dr. X, until finally he just "is" the embodiment of the projection, and the patient's capacity for the symbolic *as if* experience is absent. Mirror transference, idealizing transference and archetypal transference thus can all be experienced in an illusional or delusional way.

Similarly, the analyst can react to his patient with not only an illusional but a delusional form of countertransference. This occurs whenever an unconscious *folie à deux* takes place between analyst and analysand.

To give a personal example, not long after I had opened my practice an internationally important, very cultured and to my mind extremely intelligent man came to see me for analysis. He displayed his wide culture and his sharp thinking, and I fell more and more into an inferiority complex since I could not understand half of what he was saying. The handy Jungian consolation I tried to give myself, that I am a feeling type and therefore must accept my inferior thinking, did not make me feel any more at ease with him. I was proud on the one hand that this man came to see me, yet at the same time I dreaded every session because I just did not feel up to it. I am such a lousy analyst, I said to myself, that he is probably soon going to leave me. On top of everything else he had previously been with a renowned senior analyst, and had left him to change over to me, a beginner at the time, because he had been impressed by a lecture I had given.

It took quite a few weeks before I became aware of my delusional countertransference. Slowly it dawned on me that if I really listened, what he was saying did not make much sense and was only faintly coherent. No wonder I could not understand him, for he uttered a lot of so-called intellectual nonsense and was to a dangerous degree cut off from his very archaic emotions. But I had been blinded by a narcissistic complex: on the one hand I was flattered that this man had left that renowned analyst to come to me, and on the other I was disappointed at not being able to live up to the expectations of my own "grandiose self," which I had projected on this man. Of course, he was a good hook for this projection, but the complex had obviously deprived me of my diagnostic sense. I had been temporarily too unconscious of my countertransference to ask myself what it might mean for the analytic situation if I experienced this man *as if* he were in a grandiose way all-knowing and super-intelligent. Also, I forgot to ask *why* this man had such an influence on my sense of self-esteem and made me feel *as if* I were utterly stupid. All this had remained completely unconscious. It is usually an unrecognized complex which lures us into a delusional countertransference situation.

Transference is in every case partly illusional since fantasy is involved which may alter "reality" or at least give it a certain coloring. Countertransference, if it is neither illusional nor delusional, can put the analyst who becomes conscious of it in touch with mutual, more or less unconscious fantasies, which may be used for the analysis in a productive way.

Alchemical drawing corresponding to the Jungian model of transference-countertransference (see above, pages 25-30). King and Queen represent the opposites; the dove (spirit) appears as potentially uniting symbol (see below, pages 106-108).
(*Rosarium philosophorum,* 1550)

4

Transference

and Human Relationship

I-It and I-Thou Attitudes

In the preceding chapters we have considered various aspects of the phenomena called transference and countertransference, particular forms of projection that occur in the analytic encounter. Bearing in mind that projection is a natural process that goes on in any relationship, for better and for worse, the question then arises: But what is *real* human relationship?

I want to offer some possible answers to this question based on the ideas of Martin Buber, particularly those expressed in his early book *I and Thou* (1922). Buber's views are neatly summarized by J. MacQuarrie in *Twentieth-Century Religious Thought:*

> There are two primary attitudes which man may take up to the world, and these attitudes express themselves in two primary words or rather combinations of words: "I-It" and "I-Thou". There is no "I" taken in itself apart from a combination with an "It" or a "Thou". The "I" which is present in the speaking of the two primary word-combinations is, moreover, different in each case. The primary word "I-Thou" can only be spoken with the whole being. The primary word "I-It" can *never* be spoken with the whole being.[52]

Many of Buber's thoughts and speculations on these two primary attitudes are not too convincing to me because his psychological knowledge does not seem differentiated enough. Indeed, to a large extent he rejects depth psychology. Nevertheless, his concept of I-It and I-Thou attitudes can be very much to the point for a psychologist reflecting about human relationship.

The I-It attitude would mean that the world and one's

fellow men are seen only as objects. This can of course take place on many different levels. People can be objects of my reflections and my criticisms, but I can also turn them into objects of my own needs or my own fears, which means that other people get *used* for one's own conscious and very often unconscious purposes. The boss of a big company might for instance use his staff as objects that he needs for the financial growth of his firm, considering people only from the point of view of their usefulness for this purpose. I-It relationships can also be for mutual benefit. I may keep up a connection with an influential man because he could be useful to my career; on the other side, the influential man likes to surround himself with people who are calculating his importance because this gives him a feeling of power. What is a king without his subjects? And yet the loneliness of the king surrounded by subjects is proverbial. In Schiller's "Don Carlos," for instance, there is a moving monologue of Philip II of Spain expressing his loneliness and his need for what is in effect an I-Thou relationship. The I-It attitude leaves something out, "can never be spoken with the whole being," and is therefore never the basis for a whole relationship.

In subtle forms the I-It relation plays its part in nearly all close connections. For a young man, for example, it might be very important that his girlfriend is beautiful and generally attractive. The I-It relation could be quite dominant, as he might unconsciously use her beauty for his own need for masculine self-esteem: He needs to feel admired and envied for having success, for being attractive to a beautiful girl. The girl is his own pride, and therefore he has to possess her. I remember one young woman who really was an exceptional beauty and who resented this very much, always fearing that men courted her just because of her beauty and not for herself. This created tremendous difficulties for her and in her relationships, and sometimes she was haunted by fantasies of having an accident that would destroy her looks. And how often does a mother use her children unconsciously, possessively, as objects of her own emotional needs which have been frustrated by her husband? Or how often is the son the object of his father's ambition?

The I-Thou attitude would involve a relation to the genuine

otherness of the other person. It would mean that I in my own totality am relating to Thou in his or her own totality. *Consciously* I may have the attitude of letting the other person live in his own right and not making an object of him for my own purposes. But how do I know this does not happen unconsciously all the same? I have to be fairly well aware of my own width and length, of my own needs, fantasies and value standards, otherwise they will get projected onto the other person who automatically becomes partly an object of my own. *To relate to the otherness of Thou, I have to know who I am.* And this would imply in general a process of differentiation between Thou and I. Psychologically speaking, it would involve taking back projections, recognizing what belongs to me and what belongs to the other person.

Buber's understanding of the I-Thou attitude is rather different. He states that observation of children and of archaic people shows that the I-Thou relation is primary and the I-It secondary. He does not seem to see the difference between mystical participation (*participation mystique*) and a mature relationship to the otherness of the other person. But as we know there is a decisive difference between unconscious and conscious relationship. At the same time there is also a link between these two experiences. Erich Neumann calls the interactions between mother and infant in the first year of life the primal relationship.[53] The infant's response to the mother is total—in this sense it would correspond to Buber's I-Thou relation. But the mother is also the object of the infant's well-being—she is the very badly needed object. However, the infant is not yet I. I-It and I-Thou are contained in the infant's reality of oneness, and this primary relationship is the basic experience, the root, for all the relationships in later life. For Buber, the I-Thou relation means immediate presence— and that might be unconscious participation *or* the conscious relation to the presence of the other person in his or her otherness. The I-It attitude means making an object of anything or anyone outside of oneself in order to think *about* it or to use it, which may happen consciously or unconsciously.

I think what Buber has in mind with these two basic attitudes is rather similar to what psychologically is called Eros and Logos. Eros is our uniting feeling-link with other people, with nature or with ourselves. Logos is our capacity to separate ourselves from the surrounding world, making it into objects in order to recognize it objectively, reflect *about* it. Any fully developed human relationship needs both principles, the relating and the knowing. Knowing in this sense means the possibility of discriminating between the common ground and the difference of I and Thou. Without knowing, there is fusion or identity but not relationship between a separate I and a separate Thou.

The Jungian analyst Rosemary Gordon has called transference a "fulcrum of analysis." She too uses Buber's model of the I-Thou and I-It and states that the working-through of the transference in analysis may lead to a shift from I-It to I-Thou. She writes: "The 'I-It' attitude . . . corresponds to transference relationship, while in the 'I-Thou' attitude a whole subject encounters or relates not to an object, but to another whole subject."[54] This statement seems to me psychologically valid, as we shall see, but takes Buber's concepts from a different angle than they were meant by him.

It is a fact that in a relationship which we term transference, the Thou as another whole subject hardly does exist as such. The other person is an object for my own needs, desires, fantasies and fears. The other does not have reality as a whole subject but is somehow the carrier of the projection of my own psychic reality. The other person is experienced as a part of myself and is not a Thou in his or her own right. It is this fact that creates most relationship problems and difficulties. A close human relationship has to be mutual to be satisfactory for both partners. I would say that every close partner or friend is also an object for one's own inner needs, otherwise the feeling of closeness does not arise. But there has to be some balance between give and take, which means that the reality of the other person as a whole subject has to be taken into account. In transference relationship the pressures of the internal needs create distortions which do violence to the existence and to the wholeness of the other person.

Let us consider an example of an acted-out transference relationship outside the analytic situation: A husband and wife have three children. One night the children are very naughty, refuse to eat and so forth. The wife shouts at them, without success; the husband gives the order that since they do not seem to be hungry they must go immediately to bed. The children obey his order. Then after a while he finds out that his wife has gone secretly into their rooms and brought them food. This infuriates him, and the fight begins.

An analysis of this incident can reveal their mutual projections or transference relationship: They always quarrel about the children and their education, and what happened that evening belongs to a typical pattern. The wife had been brought up by a very strict and authoritarian father. Her mother was also afraid of him and secretly helped the children to break his disciplinary rules. Now whenever her husband takes a firm line with the children he becomes unconsciously her own strict father, and she has to help her children secretly against him just as her mother had done. But why does the husband get so terribly angry about the good mother-heart of his wife? His mother had also done some things to his father in secret. In the little village where he grew up, she used to go to a shop and buy more than she had money to pay for, and in this way accumulated quite a debt. The husband recalled what a blow it had been to his self-esteem when the shop-owner's child, who was a schoolmate, made fun of him because of his mother's debt. He himself is overscrupulous in money matters and pays for his analysis, for instance, on the dot. So doing something secretly against the father is for him connected with a threat to his own masculine self-esteem; his wife becomes his mother, who secretly undercuts his sense of masculine pride. He says that the children won't have any respect for him because of these actions of his wife.

We can see here how both partners have to enact patterns of their own childhood in the marriage, transferring parental images onto each other. So they cannot relate in an adult I-Thou relationship and thereby come to a mutual agreement about the education of their children. For her he is the authoritarian father, and for him she is the careless and irresponsible mother. In order to come to an I-Thou relationship, both would need insight into their own unconscious pattern on the one hand and into the psychic reality of their partner on the other. As long as they are unconscious about it they distort each other's real identity.

Separating and Objectivity

Becoming conscious means for the most part *separating:* separating the qualities which belong to my own person from those that belong to my partner. I have to make my own inner tendencies—the dynamics of the relationship as felt by me—and the needs of my partner into an It, an object of some kind of reflection. I have to gain to a certain extent some objectivity about those interrelations. The I-It attitude is in this sense included in the I-Thou. The subjectivity of my partner, how it affects me and how it stands in its own right apart from me, must also be the object of my conscious awareness. Eros and Logos belong to human wholeness and therefore also to the I-Thou attitude, which according to Buber can be spoken of only with the whole being.

My inclination, therefore, is to speak of transference whenever another person is *unconsciously* experienced as I-It and not as I-Thou. Transference is for the most part unconscious. If somebody consciously makes another person into an it, using him knowingly for his own needs, I would not call that transference. There might be questionable ethics behind this attitude, but on the surface at least it is not transference. Such an attitude belongs also to our so-called reality. Everybody has more or less to be also just a function for the interests of society; we need workers who build our houses, doctors who look after our health, teachers who function as educators, and so on.

For instance, a person chooses an analyst and has to pay in the expectation of eventually feeling better. The analyst then has to function as a promotor of the analysand's well-being. In this sense, there is first a conscious I-It attitude in analysis which is not yet necessarily transference. It is a reality that one can use the help of analysis if one has neurotic difficulties. Or let's say that an analyst makes patients into objects for his own research, using them without having a relationship to their full subjective being: this could be a conscious I-It attitude, not necessarily a countertransference. But as we know, even apparently conscious attitudes may be influenced by unconscious motivations. Behind the attitude of using patients as objects for research, there might be an unconscious need to have other people completely under one's control, a fear of one's own feelings due to bad experiences on the emotional side in the past, and therefore an unconscious resistance to entering a feeling relationship. The patients would thus represent a threat, and the "conscious" research on them is unconsciously a defense against them.

Since we are all motivated by unconscious as well as conscious factors, I would say that transference exists in all close human relationships—transference in the sense that we unconsciously experience the other person as an object for our own needs. Human relationship *itself* is a general basic need which seeks objects in order to be fulfilled. We just need other people for our own sake. We even need them as objects for our own psychic growth, for the process of individuation. We need to interrelate with other people in order to constellate our complexes and so become conscious of them—otherwise we escape from real life. As Jung has rightly said, "There is no possibility of individuation on the top of Mount Everest where you are sure that nobody will ever bother you. Individuation always means relationship."[55]

But what we properly call transference is usually characterized by a larger or smaller element of unreality in our conception of the other person's full subjectivity. Transference arises from the inner unconscious need to put the other person in a certain role. In such a case my sweetheart, for example, has to be identical with the unconscious fantasy I project onto her; she may have to be my judge, my loving mother, my hated shadow, my redeemer, or even an omnipotent goddess. And my own behavior in this transference relationship has to be according to that projected fantasy.

Recall the woman with a very negative mother complex (above, pages 53-55). She had experienced her mother mainly in a frustrating way, as a sadistic persecutor of her basic need to live. Her basic fantasy, that she herself had no right to live, was at the core of her neurosis, from which she suffered very badly. But at the same time this fantasy of being an outcast gave her a certain masochistic pleasure—"happy neurosis island," as one of Jung's patients called his conscious state.[56] She therefore had a need to see the negative persecuting mother in all her surroundings.

In this woman's fantasy nobody liked her, nobody took her seriously, she was somebody to be despised. She could never keep a job for any length of time because after a few days she would get the feeling that she wasn't wanted there and that people thought she was doing everything wrong, and so she would quit the job. As a matter of fact, she was compelled to *provoke* rejection from her surroundings in order to get real proofs of her unworthiness. Of course she had to play this same game of provoking rejection with me in analysis. But here it could be interpreted and related to her earlier experiences with her mother. She could not see and relate to anybody in a more or less realistic way. Everybody was just an object of her own fear and her own neurotic need to be rejected.

I think also of another patient, a man who had a basic wish to be redeemed by a woman and freed from all the discomforts of life. Finally he actually got married. The first few months things went more or less well. He was not alone any more, his sexual impulses could find fulfillment and the wife took maternal care of his daily needs. He could even indoctrinate her with his political ideas. But soon he began to complain about her: she was intellectually not his equal since she only repeated things he had told her; she was not inspiring and therefore he could not be creative; she was just a child dependent on him, and so on. He said he wanted an inspiring woman who was intellectually his equal and who was independent. But of course his wish for her independence meant that she should be independent or dependent according to *his* needs.

He began to criticize her very sharply for not being as he wished her to be. The wife reacted with fear of his criticism, insecurity, emotional withdrawal and sexual frigidity. His demands and criticisms seemed unrealistic to her but she excused him, saying that he had a complicated, artistic temperament, and that of course life with an artist is difficult. For him the marriage became more and more like a prison—"Now I am pinned down to someone who cannot give me what I need. And this prevents me from searching for real love and real happiness with a woman who is my equal." He was concerned only about what he needed from his wife; it hardly

ever occurred to him to ask what his wife might need from
him.

It is not difficult to see that this man transferred to his wife
the role of the redeeming mother-anima who should lead him
into paradise. The anima is in reality the function of relationship between a man's ego and his inner being. But of course
the poor wife could not fulfill that demand, to his great disappointment.

In both these cases, unrealistic transference-projections reduced the other person to an It and overshadowed the possibility of a human I-Thou relationship. The latter would be
characterized by the attitude of taking the reality of the other
person into full account. But also here, in "taking the other
into full account," we can often observe a hidden transference.
There are people who seem to live only through being useful
to others, through being the objects for the needs of others.
We could say that they themselves have a need to fulfill the
imagined or real demands and needs of the other person, and
thus make themselves into an It. They fulfill the Christian
commandment, "Love your neighbor as yourself." But the
commandment does not say to love your neighbor *more* than
yourself. Just this is often the problem of such people. They
cannot love themselves in their own right. They can feel the
right to live and the meaning of life only by being useful to
others. In this way they often get misused, for naturally others
take advantage of them.

I think here of a female analysand who had idealistic no-
tions about friendship, feeling that one should give all one has
to a relationship to make it worthwhile. But when we looked
closely at her life we saw that a great number of friends had
taken and were still taking advantage of her. Whatever they
needed—emotional support, a mother confessor, an object for
sex, a babysitter or just some money—she was always immediately prepared to give it. She felt she understood their need
and the importance of its fulfillment. It was like this with all
her friends of either sex, once she considered it worthwhile to
have a relationship with them.

As a child, this woman had already been taken advantage
of by her mother. "Do this for me, do that for me, I hate
doing it, I have a terrible headache," the mother used to say.

She always had to go straight home after school to help her mother do things in the house. If she wanted to play with other children, or later on to read in her room, the mother always called her to do work for her. Doing things for herself, out of her own need, was forbidden. Her mother loved her only *on condition* that she worked for her. When she wanted to give in to her own needs as a child, this was connected to the threat of losing her mother's love. So you can see that she had to transfer the demanding mother onto her friends, with the basic unconscious feeling: They will love me only on the condition that I fulfill their needs.

It seems clear, then, that every human relationship is colored to a certain degree by transference, that is, by unconscious projections. Our relationships have to be fitted into our own "world design" (*Weltentwurf*), as the existentialists would say. The more we are conscious of ourselves, the more we can relate to the otherness of another person. But some common wavelength must exist. I at least find it much more difficult to describe a full I-Thou relationship than to talk about its distortions through transference. Since man is so terribly complex, his relationships—because they include at least two persons—are even more so. There is on the one hand always the need to communicate, to achieve a union with another person, to fuse. But there is also the opposite need: to be separate, to have one's own boundaries, one's independent freedom. These are conflicting needs in oneself. In a relationship the mutual fulfilling can be heaven, but the conflicting tendencies can be hell. There is frustration in any close relationship, and the ability both to tolerate frustration and to inflict it without too many guilt feelings belongs to a psychologically mature person.

The attempt to be true to my partner and also true to myself can be a hazardous undertaking, full of conflicting opposites. Relationship also involves suffering. The suffering can be fruitful in discovering the inner contents in oneself that are projected onto the other person. This discovery can enrich us and provide the inner resources necessary in order not to identify with the needs we want to have fulfilled by the partner; then we are able to allow the partner to exist in his or her own right and also to defend our own personal integrity against unconscious demands from the other. Two people who let each other live their own lives but still feel that they have a lot in common, that they need each other, understand each other, wish the best for each other, etc.—that would be my description of a mature I-Thou relationship. It is indeed rather rare, for to allow each other separate freedom conflicts with the need for union and fusion.

In reality a relationship usually involves a mixture of I-It and I-Thou attitudes. If the reality of the Thou can be taken into genuine consideration in decisive moments, this is already a very valuable human achievement. For instance, let's say that one person hates another. The hate may be caused by the fact that the other person frustrates an intense need. An emotional passion for another person, if frustrated, can turn into a passionate hatred. Or one hates one's rival because his very existence may cause frustration of a need such as possession of the object of one's desire, or the attainment of fame or love for oneself alone. Thus he is "the enemy," the object of one's aggression, envy and hatred. He is experienced as the bad It, and his existence gets filled with fantasies arising from one's own shadow. Sometimes the enemy has done nothing to stand in one's way, but just the fact that he exists in his otherness— such as being black, or a Jew or an Italian—provokes strong emotions of aggression. Or he might simply lead a very different life, believing different things—being a light-hearted extravert, for example—and might therefore constellate pure shadow projections. Whoever is personified as the enemy is not experienced as a whole person, but gets reduced only to those real or imagined qualities which stamp him as an object for aggression.

If I can stop and ponder in such a situation, if I can think of him as another human being with his own motives, needs and shortcomings, I might really achieve something valuable. I might become conscious of my own unconscious motives and understand why I have to reduce another person to an object for my aggression. This might lead to painful insights about my shadow, and to a realization of what belongs to him and what to me. Then the other person may still be a pain in the neck, but I can treat him more fairly, in a more adapted way. He also has less power over my emotions if I can experience him as a separate person and not just as an object that exists to do damage to me.

The enemy-image plays of course a damaging role in group and mass psychology. Very often it serves as the only possible link to bind a group together; hatred for the common enemy is the bond of the group members. This is so well known that I hardly have to give examples. The enemy-image always reduces the full reality of the enemy-group to an It. Everything the members of that group do has to be distorted to fit into the enemy-fantasy, otherwise the aggression loses its intensity and can even shift into its opposite. During World War One there was a long static warfare between the French and the Germans; soldiers on both sides were lying for months in their trenches and could observe each other. The German soldiers saw that the French were just as fed up with the war as they were, and vice versa. Each saw the enemy suffering. So they started to exchange cigarettes and greet each other, and the war was over as far as they were concerned. As soon as the senior officers noticed this, the troops had to be withdrawn. Fresh soldiers with a still-powerful enemy-image had to replace them if the war were to go on.

Empathy with the reality of other persons or other groups undercuts hatred and aggression. Therefore Buber stresses his idea of the I-Thou attitude as something decisively important for the whole society.

(*Rosarium philosophorum,* 1550)

5

Human Relationship in Analysis

The I-It and I-Thou attitudes discussed in chapter four provide a good basis for looking more closely at the psychological dynamics involved in the analytic encounter. Both attitudes, as in any relationship, play a part in the interactions between analyst and analysand, and we have now to try to differentiate between transference and genuine human relationship as they may occur in the analytic setting.

In general, we speak of human relationship when the I-Thou attitude is to a certain extent dominant, and of transference when the other person is unconsciously experienced as an It. Although the phenomenon of transference exists to a certain degree in every relationship, the term transference refers specifically to projections directed toward the analyst; otherwise we talk simply of projections. Similarly, countertransference is the term used to describe the unconscious projections of the analyst onto the analysand. Jung spoke also of *active projection* or empathy,[57] where one enters actively and consciously into the inner situation of the other person, as opposed to passive projection, in which I unconsciously "find" a part of myself that really belongs to me in another person.

With all this in mind, let us now look more closely at the impact and various manifestations of transference and human relationship in analysis.

Couch versus Chair

In contrast to Freud and even more so to contemporary psychoanalysts, Jung stressed the human relationship in the analytic situation rather than the transference and its interpretation.

We can already see this emphasis in the seating arrangement typical of Jungian analysis: analyst and analysand sit in chairs facing each other, as might two people in any relationship. The analyst is free to relate spontaneously to the human reality of his patient. He is not restricted to a certain technique; he can give his thoughts, reactions and feelings as a human being. The analysand has therefore the possibility of grasping the personality of the analyst, of observing his reactions, of having him as a Thou, a human counterpart. The analysand sits on the same level as the analyst and talks to somebody he can see. In its setting the situation is not different from an ordinary face-to-face dialogue or a discussion with a friend.

The classical Freudian psychoanalytic setting is just the opposite. The analytic situation is deliberately intended to be something entirely different from ordinary social contacts. The patient lies on a couch and has to obey the basic rules of free association. The analyst is not to be seen. The position of the analysand is that of an infant put to bed by mother or father, and intentionally so, for the infantile remnants are considered the most important contents to be brought to light. The analyst tries his best not to be a full person in his otherness, but rather a part of the patient's projections. He is put into the roles of mother, father, siblings, etc., and gets reduced to an object from the patient's past. The important new aspect of the situation is that the analyst does not enact these projections but interprets them as transference and/or resistance, and relates them to past experiences of the patient. He has learned a technique for dealing with transference and resistance, and might thus also be protected from any deeper involvement—as Freud actually wanted it. If the emphasis is laid on bringing out the transference in its purest form in order to interpret it, the psychoanalytic setting certainly serves this purpose.

In Jung's view the analysis of the unconscious centers around the interpretation of dreams, whereas in psychoanalysis it centers around the interpretation of the transference. One *could* therefore imagine that in Jungian analysis the analyst and analysand are sitting together with a mutual, conscious interest. They try together to get some insight into unconscious contents through analyzing dreams. If the dreams do not seem to show any unconscious preoccupation with the person of the analyst—and sometimes they don't—there apparently exists no transference. Both analyst and analysand respect each other for their uncomplicated collaboration, and a "growth" process may indeed be going on. The analyst is apparently experienced by the analysand as the real Dr. X, and within certain limits they may reach a good understanding of the unconscious material that comes up. A kind of sympathetic feeling of friendship between two different persons might arise where the I-Thou attitude is dominant.

But of course this rarely happens in reality. Such a situation might arise if the analysand is psychologically very mature, perhaps toward the end of a thorough analysis. But in general one can say that transference exists but is not always recognized as such. It does not always come out into the open in this low-key setting or by concentrating on dreams. If the process is taking its course, there may all the same be a positive transference underneath, in the sense that the analytic situation functions as a "temenos," a sheltered, protective place encouraging spontaneity. But I feel very strongly the importance of recognizing the transference. That does not mean that one always has to talk about it or interpret it, for at times it just has to be lived through.

But the point I wanted to make in describing such a more ideal than real situation is that bits of the transference are more difficult to detect in the Jungian setting than in the psychoanalytic one, and therefore tend to be too often overlooked. The focus on the material of the analysand may have a blinding effect on the observation of his immediate reactions during the hour and also on the observation by the analyst of his own feelings. The figure of the analyst as Dr. X sometimes never does appear in dreams. But there are usually unknown figures which give a hint about the nature of the transference situation. One has to watch for them, keeping the phenomenon of transference in mind even when it does not show openly. The Freudian psychoanalyst relates every fantasy and every dream to the transference. This sounds very forced, and often *is* forced to a certain extent. But a sensitivity toward the nuances of the transference is undeniably more developed in psychoanalysis than in analytical psychology, and the Jungian must beware of falling into the opposite, of having a blind spot where the hidden transference is concerned.

Transference and Dream Interpretation

Consider a situation where an analyst is overwhelmed with dream material. The analysand wants to tell all his dreams every session, and gives the analyst hardly a chance to make a remark. He has all this interesting material for the analyst, but the analyst is not supposed to react to it or interpret it. In some cases like this I can even observe a slight gesture of defence whenever I want to open my mouth.

Swamping the analyst with dreams may serve as a defence against the fear that the analyst might destroy the rest of the patient's self-esteem through destructive criticism. In other words, the strict authoritarian father or the destructive animus of the mother is transferred onto the analyst. The patient came for help—that was his conscious intention—and trusts his dreams to the analyst in the hope of finding a healing insight. But unconsciously the analyst gets reduced to the object of the patient's fear. He is not to be trusted because the experience of trusting another person, a Thou, was damaged by mother or father in childhood. In this way arises a kind of compromise, where bringing all the dreams to the analyst is like feeding the lion so that he won't be aggressive, keeping him quiet.

In my experience there are invariably very negative parental figures where this attitude is dominant, and one can see this also from the life-history. In such cases it is probably more important to interpret the fear of the patient, at the same time showing much understanding of it, before trying to go into the dreams.

But quite frequently we are up against the difficulty some patients have in using dreams in a productive way. The consequence is that one of the main "tools" of the Jungian analyst suddenly has little therapeutic value.

As an example, I would like to mention a twenty-eight-year-old married woman. In the beginning of her analysis, dream work was difficult. Every time we tried to penetrate the meaning of a dream, I felt the atmosphere become gradually more tense. Nothing I said brought much of an echo from her. She gave little response and as a consequence my imagination too dried up.

After this happened a few times, I decided to mention the tenseness I felt in the air; I suggested that perhaps this made it difficult for her to work on her dreams. This seemed to be quite a relief for her. She said she had difficulty in concentrating because she felt afraid of not being intelligent enough to grasp dream interpretation, but knew that she *should* understand and cooperate, and then her fear mounted that I would stop the analysis if she did not do so. That would be once again a defeat in her life. It was obvious that some complex was at work in her, namely the fear of not living up to my expectations and therefore being rejected. It was not a fear which made her cooperate better—on the contrary, it blocked her by absorbing all her attention.

This woman was suffering on every side from both an intelligence complex and a complex of inferiority. She was the youngest daughter of an intelligent, artistic and very successful father, and a compulsively pious mother. From an early age onward she lived under the stress that her surroundings were asking more from her than she was able to fulfill. She felt that she should be more intelligent, more clever, more grown up and more pious than she was, in order to be accepted and to accept herself. She lived all the time in fear of not living up to expectations and therefore felt herself of no value. In fact, her dreams showed that she was haunted by fantasies of grandeur or by situations in which people belittled her. She could not trust in the assistance of helpful inner figures because both outer and inner figures were always demanding too much from her, seeming not to love and accept her for her own sake. If they did—as her husband in reality did—she was afraid this would soon be finished because she didn't deserve it. Indeed, one of her recurrent fantasies was that her husband would be unfaithful.

Once she had a dream in which an elderly woman-friend gave her a valuable antique ring set with precious stones. She really liked that dream, and of course I was very pleased about it. We talked about the fact that this motherly figure seemed to appreciate her just the way she was, and the gift of that ring was a sign that something in her was beginning to feel she had value. I then could not refrain from speaking briefly about the ring as a symbol of the Self. That was a great mistake! The next time she came depressed, and sat silently for about half an hour. Then she said that she did not care to speak, it wouldn't help anything anyhow, and fell back into silence.

When she finally came out of what she called her stubbornness state, she could say what was really the matter. Apparently my mention of the Self threw her right into her complex. She had to think what that meant and soon decided again that she was much too stupid ever to understand this. In reality she had studied at an institute where introductory lectures on the psychology of Jung were given. While she had been attracted to Jung's psychology, she had also felt to some degree too stupid to grasp it. In this same way the positive mood of that dream was now spoiled for her because I had brought in that threatening term "the Self."

I must say here that in general I hesitate to use any psychological jargon. Animus, anima, shadow, Self, etc., are useful names for a great number of inner images and connected experiences. Jung himself said that he considers them not as concepts but as names for experiences and psychic contents. They are merely descriptions of a wide range of specific experiences. In practical therapy the specific experience or the specific conflict is the important thing that has first of all to be understood and related to. Using the psychological terms risks replacing the experience with abstract words. I shall never forget a woman patient of mine who had read Jung and many years ago had come to lectures at the Zurich Jung Institute. It was formidable to hear her talk about her "awful animus problem." It was as if her animus, with which she was unconsciously identified, were doing the talking. She knew the right words, but they were unconsciously used as a terrific resistance. The fear of being devoured or imprisoned by an overpowering negative mother figure allowed nothing to come near her, to really reach her guts.

So why had I brought up that word Self in connection to my patient? We had had a good hour of mutual understanding and of productive dialogue. I had wanted to give the appropriate value to that dream image of the antique ring. The highest psychic value is what Jung called the Self, the archetype of wholeness and the regulating center of the psyche. But as nobody really knows or can know what the Self is, the word is very suggestive. An antique ring with a precious stone is an obvious symbol for the Self. I had only wanted to express this to show the value involved. Usually, when Self symbols are mentioned in relation to a patient's material, the analyst can observe a tendency toward inflation in the patient. I felt that it might be of special therapeutic help to this woman if she realized what very valuable experiences were going on in her. Indeed, if such a dream were brought to any Jungian analyst, it would be difficult for him not to say that it symbolized the Self. On the other hand, I knew she had difficulty in listening if I spoke more than three or four sentences. The word Self was brought in too shortly and abruptly, like a sugar she could not digest. It touched her intelligence complex, and everything was lost again.

I said as much to my patient, suggesting that the intelligence complex seemed to have taken over, so that it was as if she had lost that ring for the time being; but that once she found it again, she would see that it had not changed, for a precious stone is imperishable and lasts longer than one's life and the life of many generations. I said: "It seems that something will come up in you on which you can rely, something meaning more stability and continuity." And here I was able to refrain from adding that this is really the meaning of what Jung called the Self. She understood this immediately, for she knew about her everchanging moods and always complained about her lack of security. In fact her ego was weak and she was quite unstable. In her case it really was a mistake to mention the Self. I had attempted to feed her with something good, but it went down the wrong way.

Another fear prevented her from being attentive to dream work. It was the anxious question as to whether she really had been completely honest with me. Something would then occur to her which she had not yet mentioned because of inhibitions. If I should once find out that she had not been completely open and honest, I would send her away because analysis is then of no use. I said: "It seems you conceive of me as a rigid father-confessor." After this remark, she recalled how she had always been haunted by the fear that she had not told everything to her confessor, and had sometimes scrupulously gone back to confess something more. This fear in turn stemmed from the strict Catholic upbringing by her pious mother.

These fears did not appear in the contents of her dreams but in her transference behavior. For quite a time we had to work through these complexes constellated by the transference until she could have a more open attitude to the impact of her dream material. Transference analysis was first necessary and in her case rather successful.

Another example is that of a rather emotionally immature young man who had great difficulty in taking in any interpretations. He just didn't understand or couldn't listen, or else he took every interpretation as a critical attack on himself. I decided therefore to try to satisfy his frustrated need for good parents in a more concrete and rather unorthodox way. I allowed him to telephone me every day and gently gave him real advice, as a good mother or a good father would to a child. If he wanted to go for a walk with me instead of having an hour face to face, I conceded to his wishes. There was still frustration enough for him, as his demand for good parents was enormous.

In the beginning I had to go to his place, since he had such an agoraphobia that he did not dare leave his room. With time he became secure enough to travel around if he knew he could telephone me from wherever he was. He even went out with girls and finally had an affair. By that time he felt safe enough in our relationship to begin to be aggressive toward me, and he reproached me for thinking ill of him because he had sexual intercourse. Somewhere he knew that I had a permissive attitude in these matters, but still he felt that secretly I reproved him for being free of guilt. He would say, "*I* do not feel guilty about my relationship, but I can feel how *you* disapprove of it." His fear of being attacked by me had changed to the courage to attack me.

His feeling safe enough in the transference situation to be aggressive toward me was the beginning of becoming aggressive toward his own restricting superego and of defending his right to live more freely. But he could not conceive of me as I was and form an I-Thou relationship; he still had to see me as a morally restricting father.

Thus I was put in many different roles during his analysis. First I was mainly the dangerous, attacking parent which he as an unwanted child had experienced in reality. After he could trust me enough to satisfy to a certain extent his need for good and accepting parents, he became as dependent as a child on me, who had to be father and mother. Through this experience, he was able to find the courage to date a girl. But since the restrictive side in him was still very strong, I then became the censorious father whom he had to fight for his rights. At the same time his aggressive behavior toward me was also an attempt to fight against his infantile dependence.

This man's psychic state really improved tremendously, considering that he had been in and out of psychiatric hospitals and had been treated by electroshock because of the anxieties which made him unable to work. He was with me for about five years, but during that time I could never really interpret a dream for him. He experienced dreams as terrible or happy, but he simply wasn't able to understand their meaning. Symbolic thinking remained a sealed book to him. So it was important to be able to use the roles he had transferred onto me as the basis for therapy. Interpretations I could use only toward the end, when he became able to see his projections at least partially.

Archetypal Roots of Transference

It was Jung's view that behind every complex—a grouping of related images held together by a common emotional tone—there is an archetypal core.[58] With this in mind, a question that may arise in practice is whether transference projections are personal or archetypal.

In the case discussed in the previous section, for example, the young man's personal experience had been that he was an unwanted child with bad, frustrating parents, and subsequently the whole world was experienced as hostile and a source of fear. One can understand his transference as related to his personal life-history. But why had these personal experiences made such a severe neurotic of him? It is presumably because his most basic need for good and trustworthy parents had been deeply frustrated.

Now, this basic need is an archetypal phenomenon. The primary relationship between mother and child is of fundamental importance and is symbolized in the collective by the image of a positive mother-goddess—think of Isis with the Horus child, the Virgin Mary with little Jesus. If the basic need of an infant is frustrated to a large degree, the *negative* mother-goddess gets constellated. This means that life, other people and even one's own inner nature are experienced as hostile—one is worth nothing and has no right to live, so that whatever one does makes one feel guilty. Such people live under the dominance of the destructive Great Mother. This is their archetypal situation, which takes different forms in each life according to specific personal temperaments and particular personal experiences.

Although the desire and nostalgia for a good mother is archetypal, this basic need can be completely buried due to destructive experiences in early life; the person may then retire from any relationship and there is hardly any possibility of reaching him. If he can still feel the need for the good mother there is usually a better prognosis, since this may be transferred to the analyst. But then of course the fear of dangerous and painful rejection and the threat of the destructive mother-goddess get transferred too. In the case mentioned above, the young man developed the strength to fight against the guilt feelings which tried to prevent him from satisfying his natural needs of relating to a girl and having sex; he could project the moral persecutor on me and try in an aggressive way to convince me of his right to fulfill his needs.

I would say therefore that transference always has its archetypal roots, always has to do with instinctual needs and their related fantasies. After all, Freud's Oedipus situation is also archetypal. The very phenomenon of transference is itself archetypal. If a patient can experience a male analyst to a large extent as a positive mother, this must have to do with the archetypal Great Mother and the feeling of being safe in her arms. Otherwise it would be only the real, personal mother who could fulfill this role. Through transference the analyst can become a symbol of the Great Mother, and the desire to be carried and nourished by her can be experienced to a certain degree. So although transference is essentially archetypal, the archetypes manifest in specific personal circumstances; basic archetypal needs for the development of the child can be distorted by prohibitive or frustrating experiences in the outer world.

Now, in interpreting transference one can put the accent on the personal experiences of the past—this is the general Freudian procedure—or one can draw attention to its possible purpose: What does it mean for the psychic healing process that a particular kind of transference is produced by the unconscious in the specific analytic situation? The psyche apparently wants to compensate something through the transference, and so an archetype gets constellated involving analyst and analysand. Of course we need both views, but whichever standpoint we choose for interpretation and for the analytical dialogue must be based on the state of consciousness of the analysand and on his or her particular situation.

In my experience it seems important to begin work on a level which is relatively near ego-consciousness, relating unconscious material to the personal experience of the patient. An explanation of the *archetypal* situation may often be understood only intellectually, or it may lead to inflation, if it is not linked to specific and personal emotional experiences.

Earlier I suggested that the Jungian face-to-face setting in the analytic situation can have an impact on the expression of the transference. If the analysand is lying on a couch doing free association and not seeing the analyst, fantasies and thoughts about him may come out more easily. Face to face it is more difficult for the patient to talk directly about the way he perceives his analyst, just as in ordinary social contacts we are in general not used to telling someone else what we are really thinking about him. Since the Jungian setting resembles that of ordinary interactions between friends and acquaintances, certain topics may thus be avoided without this being noticed by the analyst and sometimes the analysand. In any conversation we choose to say certain things while consciously or unconsciously suppressing thoughts or feelings that do not seem adequate to the situation or appropriate to our self-image. The armchair-setting has many advantages, but it is good to know also of its disadvantages. We therefore have to be more perceptive in order to detect hidden transference phenomena. Dreams may of course give hints—but so may the way a patient offers his hand, how he can bear silences, and what topics he evades or leaves immediately once they are touched.

Countertransference and I-Thou Relationship

A most important matter is the analyst's sensitive awareness to how the patient affects him—what he feels before the patient comes, while he is there and when he leaves.

Here the analyst can develop, as mentioned before, an "instrument" with which to detect what the patient expects, and in what role he unconsciously needs to experience the analyst. This leads also to an awareness of the nature of the countertransference, which may at the same time falsify the situation; and the capacity to differentiate to a certain degree which is which is of course a most important instrument for an analyst to have.

I think of one analysand who after a year and a half of analysis suddenly obtained an interesting, difficult and demanding job in which he felt insecure. Consciously he appealed to me to help him deal with this. When he came to the next few sessions, he invariably took the telephone in my waitingroom and began a lengthy telephone conversation. When I came to call him for the hour he still had not finished, and I had to wait for him quite a while. This irritated me more and more and I began to reflect on my feelings of irritation.

Generally, I allow my analysands to use their time with me as *they* want. I do not set rules, but interpret or at least observe what comes out in this freedom. Yet this time I became irritated. What did this mean? It was of course a countertransference reaction. A pure I-Thou relationship would probably have involved the attitude: Let him telephone if he feels he has to—for the moment it seems more important to him than using his hour otherwise, so why not? Then I realized that I was angry about his lack of respect for my position and my time—for my importance.

I could have worked out the frustration of my countertransference-need to be important for him, and then—when he got off the phone—proceeded to discuss his problems and dreams with him. But in this way I felt we would have lost important insights into his unconscious state. Somewhere, half-consciously, he must have realized that his behavior could be irritating to me. Considering what I knew of his psychology, I did after all seem to be a figure important enough for him to want to annoy. So the next time it happened I told him I found it quite annoying and asked *why* he had to do this? He said he had had to make a very important phone call in connection with his new job, to somebody he couldn't reach before. Okay, I said, but *every time?*

Our discussion of his behavior revealed that he had to demonstrate to me how important *he* had become through his new job. He had become inflated, probably as a defence against the insecurity this job involved for him, and indeed would for anybody who took it on. His job was a kind of social work in which he looked after teenagers who had run away from home, used marijuana and LSD and did not want to go to school or do any work. This work fascinated him, but he felt at the same time very uncertain about what to do with these youngsters. His telephone calls showed also that he had unconsciously identified with them and their anti-authoritarian behavior. He was insecure about what stand to take and had become unconsciously infected by them; and now he had to act out this newly-acquired unconscious infection in his relationship to me. Clearly, if I had taken my irritation as belonging only to my own frustrated needs, an important piece of his analysis would have been lost.

The way in which such feelings of irritation in the analyst are used in the analytical discussion must depend on the existing relationship. A "pure" transference interpretation would probably lead the analyst to ask: "Could it be that somewhere you have the feeling of wanting to annoy me by making me wait because of your telephone conversations?" Here the analyst would be apparently objective, standing fast, far beyond the human weakness of actually getting annoyed. I do not particularly care for this so-called technique of using the countertransference. But in certain cases patients have to be left in the projection that the analyst is invulnerable and unaffected no matter what they do, otherwise they would feel terribly insecure. This technique may then be of value, and in fact it is virtually the only therapeutic tool of classical psychoanalysts. It is also true that being honest about oneself can sometimes put too much weight on one's patients.

In the case of this analysand, there was enough of an I-Thou relationship to say the following to him directly: "I have been pondering the question of why your telephone calls and your making me wait irritate me. I wonder whether it has only to do with myself. Could it not also reflect a need you have to demonstrate something to me?" In this way we started a discussion about the possible motives of his behavior. He became conscious of his inflation and his identification with the youngsters, and could then deal with it from a different point of view. One could even say that the unconscious purpose in thus demonstrating his inflation was to get free of it through analysis; that is, he unconsciously created an opportunity for me to confront him with the implications of his behavior.

In this example the difference between transference-countertransference and human relationship can be seen quite clearly. In an I-Thou relationship, where I take my partner seriously, I owe him my honesty; I can tell him how his behavior affects me. I do not have to play the invulnerable one, I can react as a human being. But in the analytic situation, of course, I would not reproach a patient for irritating me. I would take my reaction as a sign of the unconscious dynamics playing between us and try together with him to elucidate them. In this sense we are both in analysis, as Jung stated quite often. In this way I am not the superior being whom one has to keep waiting in order to show one's own importance. The analysand can conceive of me as another human being who takes him and his actions seriously. My honesty can constellate his honesty, and so we can look together into the unconscious motives which lead to transference behavior. The accent is thus on human relationship, and we try to discover the motives behind its distortion, whether this happens in analysis or outside. I think it is important too for the analysand to see the analyst also searching for his own unconscious motives and not just putting everything on him.

This honesty must in my opinion be confined to the material that concerns the analytic relationship and the transference-countertransference situation. General confessions of the analyst which do not belong strictly to the interactions in the specific analytical situation are useless, if not harmful. These stem mainly from an unrecognized countertransference need. I am also against outside social contacts between analyst and analysand. The danger of acting out the unrecognized, mutual transference-countertransference needs in the name of human relationship is too great and may be harmful for a thorough analysis.

In connection with this question of honesty, I think too of one young woman who suffered from a quite heavy depression. She had for a long time been stuck in an intense idealizing transference: I was seen as all-wonderful and perfect while she felt herself to be stupid and ridiculous.

From time to time she could allow herself fantasies of being a part of all the perfection I had to embody for her, but in general she felt unworthy of my "generous attention." Yet often she was flooded by intense envy of the "good life" I was having and jealousy of all my other patients who were so much more intelligent, beautiful and interesting than she. The fact that she had feelings of envy and jealousy was then in turn a proof of her bad character. She longed to come to the sessions, yet at the same time dreaded them out of fear that she would only be boring to me and would thus be rejected.

We discussed the implications behind these feelings again and again from different angles. She seemed to understand them at the time, yet at the next session she would usually be back in the same complex. It was as if a witch had put a curse on her, as in a fairytale, which compelled her to stay in depressive isolation. And whenever a child was born, in the form of a new insight, the witch came and took it away.

Since there was no movement whatsoever during a very long time, I had resigned myself to considering her as a so-called nursing case: she could not do without therapy yet was also unable to profit from it. Over the years I had grown tired of that immovable complex and the repetitions of her "I must bore you" attitude. I really did become bored and noticed that half the time during her sessions my mind wandered off, and I could not even listen properly when she was telling her latest dreams. Yet I felt that she was so much in her own rejection-complex that this probably would not matter too much.

But one day after about six months of my growing detachment I suddenly *heard* her say: "I am so boring to you and so uninteresting." It seemed to me she had said it this time in a different, more real tone of voice. Becoming attentive I asked her whether she *really* felt that this was so, and whether she felt that I had withdrawn somewhat, and if so since when. She could then tell me that she seemed to notice a certain withdrawal on my part over the last six months—"but of course I could never be of real interest to you," she added apologetically.

It thus became clear that she could truly perceive me as a real person. I felt that I wanted to acknowledge this, so I told her that I really had been bored more and more in the last six months, not by her as a person but by that complex of hers which must be terribly frustrating and boring for her as well. I openly admitted that I had lately against my will had great difficulties in being attentive, as if I had been bewitched by that complex. But then added: "As you can see, I am immediately with you again as soon as something connected to your real self comes up, like your very sensitive and true perception just now. Luckily not all of you is bewitched and has to go on seeing me as personified perfection, which in turn has to reject your whole imperfect and inferior being. As soon as you have the courage to express what you really feel, then I am spontaneously interested and alert. It just happens that way and seems to belong to our human condition."

She did grasp this differentiation of my feeling toward her and did not feel rejected in a global way. On the contrary, by her reaction I could see that she felt supported in her true and more realistic sense of identity. After this session the analysis began to move again and the rejection-complex loosened up considerably.

The Jungian stress on human relationship, on being free to react spontaneously to the needs of the ever-unique situation, on having no technique and no rules whatsoever, is really quite marvelous. It leaves complete freedom for creative encounter. But we must also be aware of the many dangers this can involve if one does not attempt to clarify as much as possible the unconscious motives that appear as transference-countertransference needs. We do not necessarily have to interpret every aspect of the transference. But we have to watch it in every case in order to find and maintain the appropriate therapeutic standpoint.

As said before, there are patients whose transference fantasies and needs are so much in the foreground that they cannot yet experience an I-Thou relationship with the analyst. In the case of the man with agoraphobia, I could not expect him ever to conceive of me as I actually am. I had to react from the point of view of whatever figures he imagined me to be. In other cases transference interpretations may be possible, and this can be deduced also from the analyst's countertransference reactions.

In general, one can say that the Jungian setting lends itself to the patient's grasping sooner or later who the analyst is. The reality of the analyst as a human counterpart is much more obvious than in the couch arrangement. His personal reactions inevitably disturb the transference fantasies, which can be both a positive and a negative factor in the analysis. As already mentioned, it can be negative in the sense that transference phenomena may remain unnoticed, and positive in that the human I-Thou relation is encouraged for both partners. If the analyst does not behave as unconsciously expected by the patient, there is at least a more immediate opportunity for realizing projections.

The alchemist and his female assistant tend the furnace, while
two angels (their spiritual equivalents) hold the phial containing the opposites (sun and moon). (*Mutus liber*, 1677)

6

Countertransference

and the Needs of the Analyst

The Analyst's Capacity for I-Thou Relationships

There are many qualities an analyst must have in order to be professionally successful, or indeed even adequate. Patience and the ability to concentrate come to mind, as does a sensitivity to what is behind what is being said. But perhaps the most important is the capacity to form what has been referred to in the last two chapters as an I-Thou relationship. To perceive the patient and relate to him in his specific otherness must surely be the analyst's decisive gift.

Often friends can give good advice or can console or strengthen people in distress. But mostly they give advice and consolation from their own point of view and in accordance with how they themselves would like to be treated. They unconsciously think that the other person must feel as they would or did in a similar situation. The whole point in the training of an analyst is to give him some insight into these facts of mystical participation. In becoming more conscious about himself, he must also become aware of how *different* people can be and how the same situation can be experienced in many different ways.

The I-Thou relation of the analyst to his analysand consists in having "one foot in and one foot out," as the saying goes. "One foot in" means the empathy, feeling oneself into the inner experience of the patient. "One foot out" means the possibility of looking at him from the outside, controlling one's empathy by relating it to the overall context of the psychology and developmental phase of the patient. Empathy alone, in spite of its utmost importance, can be misleading since one's own feeling-experiences may easily be confused with those of the patient. A wide range of inner experiences which have been differentiated seems to me essential to being a good analyst. Having experienced one's own neurosis with its anxiety, guilt-feelings and complexes can be of great advantage. But it is of course also important to have experienced the way in which one became able through analysis to cope with and outgrow at least the most troublesome parts of one's own psychology.

In order to be an analyst one has to be fairly stable and well balanced, and able to cope successfully with the manifestations of one's own neurosis. This is the meaning of the Chinese saying that a physician without his own wound is not a good physician. To have experienced what a neurosis feels like and how it can to a certain extent be outgrown is absolutely essential in acquiring a valuable and realistic empathy. A training analysis is therfore really a sine qua non for any analyst. But also general life-experience is needed. In this respect I am always reminded of a powerful passage in Jung's writings:

> Anyone who wants to know the human psyche will learn next to nothing from experimental psychology. He would be better advised to put away his scholar's gown, bid farewell to his study, and wander with human heart through the world. There, in the horrors of prisons, lunatic asylums and hospitals, in drab suburban pubs, in brothels and gambling-hells, in the salons of the elegant, the Stock Exchanges, Socialist meetings, churches, revivalist gatherings and ecstatic sects, through love and hate, through the experience of passion in every form in his own body, he would reap richer stores of knowledge than textbooks a foot thick could give him, and he will know how to doctor the sick with real knowledge of the human soul.[59]

But at the same time, to keep "one foot out" actually does require a lot of psychological knowledge in order to diagnose and evaluate the whole situation properly. In any case, the analyst needs to a high degree the capacity to relate to the otherness of his analysands. He must therefore also be as conscious as possible about the ways in which he might be using his patients as objects to satisfy his own personal needs or as objects of his own fears. In other words, he has to become aware of his own countertransference tendencies, which will, if unheeded, distort the relationship necessary for the analytic process to proceed more or less fruitfully. Recognizing the countertransference is also valuable in detecting the transference needs of the patient, as we have already discussed.

Now of course an analyst also needs patients for his own sake. His choice of profession, if it is really genuine, already means he has an inner call that must be realized in life for the sake of his own individuation process. His Self, so to speak, needs him to be an analyst, and an analyst needs people to analyze. So he is not sacrificing himself for others, for poor neurotic humanity. He derives satisfaction from this profession for his own well-being, it is necessary for his own psychic development. In this sense, patients are also objects for his own inner sake.

The Analytic Fee

The professional analyst usually needs patients also for purely practical reasons—to make a living. In the beginning, analysts often are anxious to get patients, and once they have a few they are afraid of losing them. This anxiety can stimulate an analyst to do the best he can for the sake of the patient. But since he is often financially dependent on the patients' continuing to come, he may also fall into too great a dependence in respect to their demands.

For instance, he may not feel free enough to allow for inevitable frustrations or to risk taking a hard line if necessary. The underlying anxiety that the patient won't come back may inhibit his freedom to relate to the analysand as the situation needs. He may try to be too nice, too understanding. And he may try to build up as quickly as possible, and sometimes forcefully, a positive transference situation in order to feel safer about the patient's continuing in analysis. If and when this happens, he is really practicing largely for his own sake. Many fears may arise from this state of affairs, such as the fear that the patient may be disappointed if the analyst does not understand his dreams properly or come up with some brilliant insight every session. The patient can thus also become an object of the analyst's own fear.

The source of this anxiety is not always well enough recognized. One's whole behavior might be rationalized by saying that it is terribly important for the *patient* to stay in analysis, and therefore one has to do all one can to keep him there. This may be so, but the legitimate need of the analyst to make his living through his patients must be conscious in order to distinguish what is what. It is also important to be fully aware of the possible need to experience one's own identity through analyzing patients.

Of course, it is not a very helpful situation when the analyst is dependent on just a few patients to make his living. With no private resources it would be wise to take a part-time job as well, in order to feel financially more secure. If this is not possible, one has to be as conscious as one can about the dangers of the situation, taking the risk and consequences of being poor for a while but being true to the necessities of the analysis. It is a fact of human reality that the analyst needs the fees from the patient for his own living. To admit this honestly to oneself is important. But it is in general not favorable for the therapy if the patient knows that the analyst is financially dependent on him, for this knowledge can be used unconsciously for power manipulations. The analyst must have a stand as independent as possible in order to build up a therapeutically valuable relationship with the analysand. Therefore right from the start he needs to trust that patients will come and stay if he works well and honestly, according to the inner truth of each analytic situation.

The beginning analyst will usually take anybody who comes along; he cannot yet choose who will be suitable for analysis in general and for working especially with him. Apart from his financial needs and the eagerness to get patients, this may also have something to do with his lack of experience. But experience usually can be gained only through painful realizations that analysis is not for everybody and that he himself cannot be a good analyst for everybody. This kind of experience probably cannot be avoided—even when it is not always to the benefit of the patient.

The whole matter of fees, indeed, is a delicate and complex-constellating issue for many analysts. Some feel it is an important part of the therapy, others doubt this. Jung had nothing to say on the subject, but Freud thought it was essential for the patient to pay a fee. At the Tavistock Clinic in London, however, one can nowadays get free analytic treatment, even from classical psychoanalysts, and the ones I have spoken to there claim this has no negative side-effects on the course of the analysis. In England, at least, the collective consciousness seems to have changed in this respect. People have to pay quite a sum every week to the National Health Service, and for this they get medical treatment practically free of charge when they need it. So they may feel they also have a right to free analytic treatment, and do not feel guilty about taking the analyst's time and not giving him money in return. In Switzerland and in the United States it is different. Some fees for psychiatrists are covered by health insurance; the patient may have to pay a part of it, but he at least knows his doctor is being paid.

The belief that it is important for the patient to pay fees might be a rationalization for the fact that *the analyst* needs the fees from the patient. This need may raise some guilt-feelings—after all, what kind of an I-Thou relationship is this, if one partner wants to get paid for it?

But the analyst too has to live. His training was expensive and he may have accumulated debts; he may have a house, a mortgage, a family to support, and he too has to buy groceries. My feeling is that it is not to the benefit of his work to be prey to resentments about sacrificing his time, energy and knowledge solely for the love of mankind. I also still believe it is important for the *patient* to pay a fee because money symbolically is energy: we exert our energy to earn money, and we put our money where our energy wants to go.

The question of how large a fee to charge may itself be a matter for some soul-searching. How much is adequate? What is appropriate? One analyst charges "what the market will bear," another what he feels his own energy is worth to him, someone else what the patient can afford. I know of one analyst who says simply that his energy for analysis is not constellated if he is not paid a substantial fee.

If the fees are much too low, or nothing at all, that can mean to the patient that the analyst is *in fact* a good mother, or someone to be grateful to. Resentment at having to be grateful may be felt but have to be suppressed—after all, one cannot be aggressive toward such a nice person who is trying to do so much good. Naturally this may also inhibit the possibility of an honest I-Thou relationship. Such fantasies may arise anyhow, whether the patient pays a fee or not. But then they can be interpreted as transference phenomena as distinguished from outer reality. Money may symbolize many things, but it is after all a factor of our daily lives. If a patient does not pay or pays too little, he really does feel more dependent on his analyst and experiences himself in an infantile situation.

Especially at the beginning of his practice an analyst may have problems regarding fees. He often has the need to be loved by his patients in order to feel secure in his work and at ease with himself, and the fee may stand in the way of this. He might think: "The less I charge, the less the patient will feel resentments against me. He will trust me more because he will see that I am not interested in his money but in him as a human being." These are countertransference reactions which often have little to do with the reality of the patient. Behind them can be the unspoken plea, "Please come to me and stay with me, I am here for you. Let me be helpful, it doesn't cost you much. I need to be your loved companion who tries to help you."

But what about money as a symbol for value? If an analyst charges too little, the patient may get the feeling that his analysis has little value or that something is wrong with the status of the analyst. As said before, the patient may have a feeling of gratitude for such generosity, but also resentment about having to feel grateful. This resentment may be defended by thinking, "The analysis is not worth much—what use does it have?" Money as a symbol of value can also have an impact on the analyst. He may ask himself, "Are the hours I give worth all the money the patient has to pay? What is my worth as an analyst?"

The matter of fees thus often has something to do with the conscious or unconscious self-evaluation of the analyst. In the beginning analysts typically feel more insecure and have therefore a tendency to charge too little. Sometimes, however, in overcompensating their insecurity they may also charge too much. It is also a fact that patients who pay a large fee are often experienced by the analyst as a greater threat than those who pay less. He may somehow imagine that high-paying patients have much greater expectations of him. This too can be a phenomenon of countertransference. His own ego-ideal or inner ideal analyst threatens him with the fear of being inadequate and not worth all that money; and this inner fear may get projected or countertransferred onto the patient. It is often true that rich people who can pay a handsome fee do expect all the best that money can buy; and they can of course transfer those expectations onto the analyst together with their right of criticism. But here is just the place for the analyst to step in, showing that psychic health cannot be bought so easily and that the reality of the psyche has different values, instead of unconsciously falling into the trap. Indeed, probably he will have to take this line in any case, if only in self-defense.

I do not think that serious analysts invest less libido and interest in patients who pay little than in those who pay well. But high fees may represent a much greater threat to an analyst, as he will have to show himself worth this money. He may even be a better analyst to those who pay little, because he feels more at ease. I think one has to be conscious of these seemingly banal factors, since they may very much color the relationship and the transference-countertransference. One should charge neither more nor less than what one can swallow oneself.

It goes without saying that the fees have to be flexible in order to meet the real situation of the patient. I think it is valuable to have a standard fee according to general custom and according to one's own conscious self-evaluation, one's standard as an analyst. This can then be adapted to individual needs. I usually tell analysands my standard fee, and if they cannot pay it, I tell them on what grounds I would take them into analysis anyway or on what grounds I cannot take them. I tell those who can pay only a low fee that once their financial circumstances change for the better, I am going to charge more. One has to be careful that the feeling of having to be grateful does not do harm to the analysis. Of course once a relationship is established one can more easily discuss these matters if they involve problems. So far I have been able to withstand the temptation to charge a much higher fee to rich people. I think it is important that they do not get the feeling of having the power to buy the analyst.

I experienced how the fee can play a part in analysis with one patient, a severe compulsive with greatly inhibited aggression. It was not possible to get near him, and he had horrible dreams which showed that his defences were not without reason. Hardly anything moved for a long time, and I felt quite worn out with this case. I could not stop the analysis, for that would have caused him a dangerous degree of anxiety. I felt as a matter of fact that he would have to go to a woman analyst if anything at all could be done and had suggested this to him, but he was afraid to face the change. The problem for me was my conviction that he could not profit from further analysis with me, but that any suggestion of this on my part would be taken as a rejection. So I had to find a way for *him* to reject *me*. In the event that happened quite instinctively.

I decided to raise the fee to the normal standard—he had been paying too little—and simply put the higher fee on my bill, sending it to him without discussing it in the hour. If he did not come any more, I thought, all the better for him and for me. He could blame *me* for it and much less damage would be done than if I had to tell him to stop. Being a compulsive, he had of course the custom of paying his bills on the dot—but this time he did not pay and did not telephone to arrange another hour. For a compulsive it is already an achievement if he can overcome his guilt at not paying his bills immediately. He paid the bill by postal order more than a month later, and after a while he telephoned to arrange for further hours.

In the third hour he was finally able to come out with his anger toward me for having raised his fee; he had needed all this time to get up his courage. Then he was able to let out further aggression, telling me that he would not mind paying a higher fee if things were moving—that is, if I were a better analyst. This was really a great achievement. Now I could discuss with him why I thought he would profit more from working with a woman. I referred him, and he actually had the courage to telephone and go to her.

The Need for Therapeutic Success

There can be another need of the analyst which he sometimes unconsciously wants the patient to satisfy. This is the need for psychotherapeutic success—that is, a substantial improvement in the psychic health of the patient. Candidates at training institutes are very often anxious for success in order to be recognized as suitable and gifted for this profession by the control analysts. In general, analysts may fear for their reputations if they treat people without success. The patient thus becomes an object for enhancing the analyst's reputation.

Now of course nothing need be said against therapeutic success—after all, the patient wants to get better, and usually the analyst has the same wish for the patient in a legitimate way. Improvement through analysis is a legitimate satisfaction for both partners, and is indeed the aim of analysis as a form of psychotherapy. Consciously a Jungian analyst has usually adopted the attitude that the work succeeds only *Deo concedente*—God willing—as Jung often stressed.[60] For just this reason his need to use the patient as a proof of his own abilities may get repressed and stimulate countertransference phenomena from the unconscious. He may feel strong unconscious resentments against the analysand for not improving, and thus he may become overactive, didactic, demanding or impatient.

In other words, if an analyst becomes aware of resentments against a patient who does not seem to be getting better, it is important to reflect on those feelings as signs of countertransference. His own frustrated need to prove himself a successful analyst, or his own guilt-feelings, may be involved.

Earlier I suggested that a countertransference reaction might also be an answer to an unrecognized transference content of the analysand. It is therefore valuable to ask not only about one's own unconscious motives but also about the unconscious situation of the patient. Perhaps there is a tendency or complex in the patient that needs to experience the analyst as demanding and impatient, like the familiar image of mother or father, so that he unconsciously provokes the analyst *really* to fit these transference-images. If this is not recognized, an old pattern may simply be repeated. The patient may feel overburdened by the demands of the analyst—the way it always was in his life—and retire to a resigned attitude. Or he may have feared that he would lose the love of the analyst or that in time the analyst would get fed up with him, just as other people did before—and then as soon as the analyst shows a sign of impatience, there is the proof that it will always be that way.

We must never forget that in everyone there are strong forces *against* change, complexes that resist any interference with the old familiar pattern. They try to kill everything new and distort it back into the old scheme. In mythology and religion the survival of the divine child, an archetypal symbol for future possibilities, is always threatened by the "old guard." Such resistance to change regularly plays a great part in transference phenomena. The analyst is to be fitted into the old scheme—and then everything can stay as it always was. Images of resistance may come up in dreams, but even there they are not always recognized fully enough in the interpretation if the analyst does not think of them. Watching one's countertransference reactions, differentiating them to see what belongs to the analyst and what might be being provoked unconsciously by the patient, is indispensable in detecting these things.

Regarding resistance coupled with fear of the unconscious, I must give the last word here to Jung himself:

> There is good reason and ample justification for these resist-
> ances and they should never, under any circumstances, be
> ridden over roughshod or otherwise argued out of existence.
> Neither should they be belittled, disparaged, or made ridicu-
> lous; on the contrary, they should be taken with the utmost
> seriousness as a vitally important defence mechanism against
> overpowering contents which are often difficult to control. The
> general rule should be that the weakness of the conscious
> attitude is proportional to the strength of the resistance. When,
> therefore, there are strong resistances, the conscious rapport
> with the patient must be carefully watched, and . . . his con-
> scious attitude must be supported to such a degree that, in
> view of later developments, one would be bound to charge
> oneself with the grossest inconsistency. . . .
> Nor is it beside the point to add that consistent support of

the conscious attitude has in itself a high therapeutic value and not infrequently serves to bring about satisfactory results. It would be a dangerous prejudice to imagine that analysis of the unconscious is the one and only panacea which should therefore be employed in every case.[61]

Power, Curiosity and Possessiveness

Besides the need for therapeutic success there are in the analyst many other general human needs that seek fulfillment through his professional life. If he does not pay constant attention to them, they may enter by the unconscious back door into the countertransference. It can also work the other way around: being sensitive to possible countertransference reactions may reveal to him his own unrecognized tendencies.

The power-drive, for instance, expresses an important human need to build up one's ego and find one's adequate place in society. It is of course also working in the analyst and in the analytic situation. Patients often have a tendency to become dependent on their analyst and thus project a lot of power onto him. He becomes the source or support of their emotional and spiritual life, and they can hardly bear it if he takes a vacation or when they have to leave him after the hour. Apart from the burden of such situations, the analyst may also enjoy his importance, using his patients as objects to satisfy his own need for power. If he is conscious of his enjoyment of power and gives it its proper place, why not? But from the point of view of the inner ideal analyst, such a feeling would be experienced as somehow false or unethical, and therefore tends to be repressed. It can then show itself as countertransference, for instance in being overprotective, giving a lot of extra time to certain patients, even doing things for them which are apparently too difficult for them to do themselves yet. In this way he may unconsciously keep them much longer than necessary in a state of dependence; he may rationalize his actions as a therapeutic need of theirs, when in reality his own power-need is at stake.[62]

An analyst may also experience anger if a patient does not follow a course that has been discussed in analysis, or if he goes around asking all kinds of other people for advice and opinions concerning his problems. Of course this shows that the analysand cannot "keep the vessel closed," as the alchemists would say—the vessel here being the analytic temenos—and the analyst may rightly be annoyed since this may harm the analytic process. This would have to do with his genuine concern for the patient. But real *anger* would more likely indicate his own resentment that the patient does not behave as he expects him to; that is, he cannot accept what the patient does as belonging to the actual psychic state of the patient. He may be frustrated at not having all the power he wants over the patient, and if this power-countertransference does not get recognized, he may moralize at length about the therapeutic importance of the alchemical vessel.

Here again, recognizing the frustration of his own power-need can lead the analyst to the question of why the patient unconsciously has to provoke this. Elucidation of the motives and psychological dynamics behind the behavior of the patient might be the result, instead of an angry moralizing attitude on the part of the analyst.

Unconscious possessiveness also belongs here. This may show itself in feelings of jealousy on the part of the analyst: "He is *my* analysand, I want to treat him and form him—and nobody may interfere with that!" One might call this a Pygmalion or savior complex. Such feelings too can be rationalized by pushing the patient's need for therapy into the foreground. For instance, an analysand might have legitimate reasons for wanting to change over to analysis with someone else. His analyst may tell him, "Of course I can see that such a change might be good for you in time. But for the moment I feel that the specific attitude of that person could do harm. It is still too early." Or under the auspices of the so-called frank and spontaneous relationship with the analysand, he could even say, "Why do you want to go to *that* analyst? Can't you see that he isn't Jungian enough (or too orthodox a Jungian, or anima-possessed)?" Perhaps this is at least an honest, straightforward jealousy-reaction, though not very ethical or fair to the reputation of the colleague. But behind the best of conscious intentions—it wouldn't work, is therapeutically wrong, and so forth—there may lurk the unconscious need to hold on to one's analysand.

There may also be resentment in the analyst if he discovers that the patient does not disclose everything to him. He may tell things to other people and not to his analyst, who then feels hurt by this apparent lack of trust; the analyst's own need to be all-trustworthy is frustrated by the patient. He may then reproach the patient, instead of taking it as a transference-symptom to be analyzed.

A few words can also be said about the analyst's curiosity. It is in the nature of his daily work to hear details of the patient's intimacies, his sex life and involvement with other people the analyst may know, learning many things about many people which he would not otherwise. He thus can use his patients to get intimate "news of the world." This might really be a reward of his profession, for who is not curious? The danger could be that he uses the patient's time to get information which does not really concern the analysis. However, perhaps this does fundamentally less harm than the repression of curiosity. If curiosity is repressed as being low and unethical for an analyst, it can cause false inhibitions. Whenever the analyst's curiosity comes up he may become afraid that the patient will think he is indiscreet. The fear of his own curiosity thus gets countertransferred to the patient. In this way the analyst may feel uneasy whenever a painful intimacy or a piece of gossip comes up. In general, the disclosure of certain intimacies is usually painful for the patient because he fears the disapproval of the analyst. Transference and countertransference can thus cause a tendency to avoid certain topics which might be important for the analysis.

Another countertransference danger may be the unrecognized need of the analyst to live through his patients those sides of life which he himself cannot or does not live. Patients can be a source for information, for relationship, for bringing color and juice, pain and suffering into the life of an analyst, and they make him feel important and useful and alive. This can become for the analyst a substitute for living his own life. Of course analysands belong very much to the life of an analyst. But if they become overly important to his feeling of being alive, they may unconsciously be used as countertransference-objects. As a revenge he can secretly burden them with his own possessiveness. Here there arises unhealthy phenomena of mutual dependence instead of genuine human relationship.

In view of the extremely complex and subtle work that an analyst has to do, one can never stress enough the importance of being honestly in touch with oneself. This implies also that the analyst lead as full a life as is genuinely agreeable to his whole personality. To actively pursue his hobbies, do scientific or artistic work which interests him, have relationships with friends and with nature, have a satisfying sex-life, take vacations and generally enjoy himself—all this may take time and energy away from his patients, but in the long run will contribute to his effectiveness as an analyst. After all, if one does not know how to live, how is one ever going to constellate this knowledge in analysands?

7

Erotic Love in Analysis

We come now to the emotionally most intense form of transference—transference-love and its connected sexual needs—
and how this may affect the analysis.

It goes without saying that countertransference-love may
also arise in the analyst in a more or less intense form. It may
even happen that the mutual emotions become so strong that
a concrete sexual relationship seems to be indicated. This puts
a heavy weight of responsibility and conflict on the analyst.
He has to consider carefully his own inner situation, his motives as well as those of his analysand. Some successful mar-
riages have indeed arisen out of an analytic situation. But if
the decision is made for a concrete relationship, analysis as
such cannot continue, except of course with another analyst.
Analysis and a concrete love relationship do not go together,
although the latter can be a fuller experience and might have
even more impact on the individuation process.

There are many reasons why analysis and a love relationship between the same partners is not only inappropriate but
can do harm to both. In the first place, collective consciousness in our society and in our profession condemns a concrete
love relationship between analyst and analysand. Now an analyst may feel this to be an outdated superego attitude, and
believe that individuation actually means not to identify with
collective moral standards but to adapt them to genuine situations in real life. On this basis he might make a personal
decision to act out the emotional attraction. But at the same
time he and his analysand have to live in our society, and the
decision to be both analyst and lover would inevitably put a
lot of strain on their relationship. The collective disapproval
is so great that both would have to keep absolute secrecy.
This might at first even stimulate the mystery, for forbidden
fruit is notoriously fascinating. But in the long run there
would arise inner and outer pressures that would lead to

"It is the spirit which unites." (*Rosarium philosophorum*, 1550)

dishonesties and lies to conceal the situation in order not to ruin the reputation of the analyst. Although the collective view of these things may be based on an outdated value-system, one would have to change this in order to give more freedom to the individual decisions of analyst and analysand.

But quite apart from collective opinion and any moral or ethical considerations, the analytic relationship and physical love are too different in nature, in essence and in aim to be mingled, and there is furthermore a sound psychological basis for not combining the two.

Earlier I have referred to Jung's long essay, "The Psychology of the Transference," where in order to illustrate the unconscious dynamics behind the analytic situation he uses a series of drawings from the medieval alchemical work *Rosarium philosophorum.* Jung writes that for him this approach was the only possibility of coming to grips with such a complex and difficult field of human interaction and the only way to understand its meaning.[63]

In our present context there is something of special importance in some of these drawings. Very frequently there is a dove that carries a twig in its beak. The twig is placed in such a way that it points deeply into the event taking place in the rest of the picture. In Greece the dove symbolized the Aphrodite of heaven in contrast to the earthly Aphrodite, and this would mean spiritual, all-embracing love or *agape.* The word *agape* is used later in the New Testament to mean Christian love in contrast to worldly erotic love. The Holy Spirit also appears in the form of a dove, and is a testimony of the love which God accorded mankind after the redemption by Christ. The dove is thus associated with redemption and with love of a spiritual nature. The earthly Aphrodite stands for natural, erotic love, the result of which is the physical child.

In the third drawing of the series (opposite), where king and queen are naked for the first time, we find some written words connected to the dove: *Spiritus est qui unificat,* "it is the spirit which unites." There is also another version, which reads *Spiritus est qui vivicat,* "it is the spirit which brings to life." Jung gives still another amplification for the dove: the dove of Noah carrying a twig from the olive tree as a sign that the

Flood is over and there is peace again between God and man.[64] It is called the peace-dove, the twig symbolizing peace. Psychologically peace means a state of reconciliation, and the twig carried by the dove is therefore a reconciling symbol between God and man; we could call it a symbol of totality or of the Self. Man and God are at peace with each other again, as when Noah fulfilled the will of God.

Now all this may seem somewhat irrelevant to the analytic situation, but these images symbolize an important attitude for the analyst to have, an attitude based on an understanding of archetypal patterns in the psyche.

The attitude symbolized by the dove carrying the twig involves a kind of love that is directed toward the still-hidden totality of the patient, to the process of self-development of the person coming for help. This love is in other words directed toward a spiritual or psychic child and not a physical union. The "marriage" between analyst and analysand is therefore of a spiritual or symbolic nature.

The transference-love of the patient does not, in general, fall on the analyst Dr. X as a person. In the beginning, it is not the I-Thou relationship that is in the foreground, but rather the transference. The analyst may stimulate unconscious needs to be loved, supported and understood, as well as the need to fuse with another human being. Through transference he gets "built into" the inner images of the analysand's fantasy-life. As mentioned before, it is in fact an important aim of analysis to transform transference into an I-Thou relationship through the gradual taking-back of projections. The analysand can thereby acquire the experience of his own entity, which creates the possibility of relating to a Thou. This is easily said, but in reality it often involves a long, difficult and very painful process, one which the analyst cannot direct, but can only accompany, understand and interpret to a certain degree. In Jungian terminology, it is directed by the influence of the Self—symbolized for instance by the dove carrying the twig—and can therefore succeed only *Deo concedente,* "with the help of God," as the alchemists used to say.

The analytic relationship is essentially different from any other human relationship in that it has a particular aim. It is not a relationship for its own sake. The aim in analysis is to establish a relationship between the conscious ego and the unconscious. The presence of the analyst in his humanness is at the same time *an instrument in the service of the Self.* In his relationship to the patient the analyst has to be conscious of this role. But when the patient is overcome by strong transference-love, he or she often forgets or represses the reason for originally coming to see the analyst—namely, to do therapeutic work. The professed aim of analysis then often becomes insignificant.

For a female patient, for instance, it can become much more important that the analyst should marry her, seduce her or love her than interpret her dreams or show how her complexes disrupt her life. The full flight of erotic love demands that the analyst feel as intensely toward her as she does toward him. She may become unbearably jealous at the thought that he also sees other patients, and suffer from the idea that all the attention her beloved analyst gives her is only because she pays him, it is "part of his job." From all this can develop a muddle of resentment, love, hate and passion. The patient declares that she will not come anymore; she will punish the analyst for his apparent callousness and in any case cannot stand these frustrating emotional entanglements. However, the tie is usually so strong that she phones the same evening, excuses herself for her outburst and is present again at the next session.

Now how does such transference behavior affect the analyst? Although each situation is unique, certain countertransference patterns are common. Generally one can say that strong emotions directed toward the analyst do affect his own emotional life. He may somewhere enjoy it, or be afraid of it; guilt feelings may arise about being the cause of so much apparent distress. He may also be tempted to enter the play and fulfill the fantasies of the patient in a concrete way, and therefore has to struggle with himself. It may on the other hand be terribly irritating and annoying to be the victim of so many unwanted demands. Or it may be a satisfaction to the analyst's masculine vanity that women fall in love with him so intensely. Training candidates are often proud of themselves if they feel that they can constellate transference-love. I remember how the wife of one student with a sexual masculinity problem told everybody that her husband had a rich woman patient who telephoned him every evening, from anywhere in the world, because she had to hear his voice. It seemed important for their marriage that her husband had such an effect on a rich woman but loved only her—"What a hero of a husband I have, so much sex appeal, and he's all mine!" (In all fairness I must admit this wasn't quite her husband's attitude.)

Many of these different reactions to transference-love can be found in the analyst, and it is of course essential that he become honestly aware of them. They are countertransference phenomena that can reveal to him something about himself. But also they can give him an idea of the chord in him the patient tries to play on, what the patient unconsciously wants. If for instance he feels annoyed at her demands, this may be an indication that the patient unconsciously wants to provoke his annoyance, even though consciously she wants just the opposite. This might be a repetitive pattern stemming from early childhood, in order to prove to herself that she has no right to love, or that her love is only annoying to other people. But it might also have a deeper meaning. It might be an unconscious plea: "Please *do* get annoyed and stop my overwhelming demands. I don't have the strength to do this myself, I need you to put your foot down." We must not forget that to let oneself be overwhelmed by transference-love often represents a resistance against the process of self-development. To stay in an infantile state of dependence might be in part rewarding. It might be easier to telephone the analyst in the middle of the night, just to hear his voice, than to endure one's loneliness and paint a picture or write down one's thoughts and emotions.

Now, in terms of our symbolic picture, the analyst is in the service of the dove, the potential wholeness of the patient. The infantile shortcomings, needs and dependencies belong to it and have to be accepted. Of course the analyst is interested in stimulating the patient's capacity eventually to work them through; but often they just have to be lived with and contained as part of the transference for a certain time. One has to encourage all feelings in order to set a limit to them later on. They may have to be sacrificed sooner or later—but not repressed—in order for the personality to grow. In my experi-

The union of opposites as an inner, spiritual process, symbolized by king and queen with wings. (*Rosarium philosophorum,* 1550)

ence, if patients can see their transference-love as a painful but potentially creative suffering—the fire which transforms the *prima materia* in the alchemical vessel—the process can take a deeply worthwhile course. It constellates the dove in the analytic marriage, and the encounter can be astonishingly creative.

If patients identify *completely* with their transference-love and their wish for a concrete sexual relationship, it is usually a sign of resistance. It is very important that the analyst not give in to their demands, for this could cause the deepest disappointment in the patient or bring out terrible anxieties. It is of course important to accept the patient's feelings as genuine, and to express one's real empathy for and understanding of his or her situation. But in spite of all the attempts at seduction, the patient usually feels more secure if he or she can rely on the analyst's strong stand, his capacity to hold the tension.

Sometimes an analyst may rightly feel that it would be the

best thing therapeutically if the need for a more complete relationship could be fulfilled. A really satisfying sexual relationship can indeed be most valuable and more rewarding than any amount of therapy. But the analyst must not attempt to provide this, for as soon as he does he abrogates the instrumental role he has taken on in the psychology of the patient, and the birth of the divine child, so to speak, is abruptly aborted. To make love to someone for professedly therapeutic reasons is in any case essentially abhorrent to the instincts, nor is it *really* what the patient wants, no matter what he or she says. Because it is in the nature of the transference that the analyst is not seen as a real separate person, and because of what is at stake for the patient, the analytic relationship and sexual love cannot go together.

The implications of the erotic transference-countertransference thus put a heavy weight of responsibility on both parties. This is true in any form of analysis, but especially where the analyst is trained as a Jungian, with no clear-cut technique for handling it. Virtually his only defence is a firm standpoint regarding the purpose of the analytic encounter — the conviction that however the relationship may manifest, whether in passionate and demanding overtones or in a mutually considerate respect that characterizes the genuine I-Thou relationship, his function is to serve the dove, the process of individuation.

This aim, inevitably, includes the paradox of both living one's nature and working *against* nature; for the process of becoming conscious is often, as Jung points out, an *opus contra naturam:* "It goes against nature not to yield to an ardent desire."[65] It is specifically the essence of human nature to want to become conscious, while the raw forces of nature itself want *not* to become conscious. This is the paradox that must be faced by anyone who takes on the task of truly becoming what he or she potentially is.

In the final analysis, the analytic encounter is both a challenge and an opportunity, and the way in which analyst and analysand deal with their emotional interactions has a significance extending far beyond the boundaries of any particular relationship. This can at least be some consolation in the midst of what is often a problematic situation. As Jung writes:

Individuation has two principal aspects: in the first place it is an internal and subjective process of integration, and in the second it is an equally indispensable process of objective relationship. Neither can exist without the other, although sometimes the one and sometimes the other predominates. This double aspect has two corresponding dangers. The first is the danger of the patient's using the opportunities for spiritual development arising out of the analysis of the unconscious as a pretext for evading the deeper human responsibilities, and for affecting a certain "spirituality" which cannot stand up to moral criticism; the second is the danger that atavistic tendencies may gain the ascendancy and drag the relationship down to a primitive level. Between this Scylla and that Charybdis there is a narrow passage. . . .

Looked at in this light, the bond established by the transference—however hard to bear and however incomprehensible it may seem—is vitally important not only for the individual but also for society, and indeed for the moral and spiritual progress of mankind. So, when the psychotherapist has to struggle with difficult transference problems, he can at least take comfort in these reflections. He is not just working for this particular patient . . . but for himself as well and his own soul, and in so doing he is perhaps laying an infinitesimal grain in the scales of humanity's soul. Small and invisible as this contribution may be, it is yet an *opus magnum*. . . . The ultimate questions of psychotherapy are not a private matter—they represent a supreme responsibility.[66]

Notes

CW — *The Collected Works of C.G. Jung*

1. See Michael Fordham, "Notes on the Transference," in M. Fordham et al., *Technique in Jungian Analysis;* also Fordham, *Jungian Psychotherapy,* and Kenneth Lambert, *Analysis, Repair and Individuation.*
2. See essays by R. Blomeyer and Hans Dieckmann, "Die Konstellierung der Gegenübertragung beim Auftreten archetypischer Träume."
3. Jung, "The Tavistock Lectures," in *The Symbolic Life,* CW 18, pars. 349, 351. (These lectures are also available separately as *Analytical Psychology: Its Theory and Practice,* Pantheon Books, New York, 1968.)
4. Ibid., par. 306.
5. Ibid., par. 331.
6. Ibid., par. 337.
7. Jung, "The Psychology of the Transference," in *The Practice of Psychotherapy,* CW 16.
8. Ibid., p. 164.
9. Jung, *Aion,* CW 9ii, par. 25.
10. Jung, "The Psychology of the Transference," CW 16, p. 165.
11. Ibid., par. 367.
12. Jung, "Psychic Conflicts in a Child," in *The Development of Personality,* CW 17, p. 7.
13. Jung, "The Realities of Practical Psychotherapy," in *The Practice of Psychotherapy,* CW 16, par. 543.
14. Ibid.
15. Letter of 14 January 1946, in Gerhard Adler and Aniela Jaffé, eds., *C.G. Jung Letters,* vol. 1, p. 405.
16. Freud, "Studies on Hysteria," in *Collected Works,* vol. 2.
17. Ibid., pp. 307ff.
18. Ernest Jones, *Sigmund Freud: Life and Work,* vol. 1, p. 247.
19. Freud, "Recommendations to Physicians Practising Psycho-Analysis," in *Collected Works,* vol. 12, p. 115.
20. Freud, "General Theory of the Neuroses," in *Collected Works,* vol. 16, p. 444.

21. Jung, "The Relations Between the Ego and the Unconscious," in *Two Essays on Analytical Psychology,* CW 7, pars. 206-208.

22. Jung, "The Psychology of the Transference," CW 16, pars. 353ff.

23. See Erich Neumann, *The Child,* and Eric Erikson, *Childhood and Society.*

24. Jürg Willi, *Die Zweierbeziehung,* p. 71.

25. Jung, "The Psychology of the Transference," CW 16, pars. 422ff.

26. At each end of the top line, where I have put the ego of patient and analyst, Jung has adept and soror (terms for the alchemist and his female assistant); and on the bottom line where I have the unconscious of each, Jung has anima and animus. I have also changed the lettering on the lines to simplify the references in the discussion.

27. See Jung, "Definitions," in *Psychological Types,* CW 6, par. 784.

28. Ibid., pars. 741, 781.

29. Neumann, "Disturbances of the Primal Relationship and their Consequences," in *The Child* (chapter 3).

30. Mario Jacoby, "A Contribution to the Phenomenon of Transference."

31. Erich Neumann, "Zu Mozarts Zauberflöte," in *Zur Psychologie des Weiblichen.*

32. See Jung, "Definitions," in *Psychological Types,* CW 6, par. 781.

33. Ibid., pars. 738ff, 783.

34. Jung, *The Practice of Psychotherapy,* CW 16, pars. 1, 544.

35. Freud, "The Future Prospects of Psycho-Analytic Therapy," in *Collected Works,* vol. 11, pp. 44ff.

36. See P. Heimann, "On Counter-Transference," and A. Reich, "On Counter-Transference."

37. See Kenneth Lambert, *Analysis, Repair and Individuation.*

38. M. Fordham et al., *Technique in Jungian Analysis,* pp. 137ff.

39. Ibid., pp. 142ff.

40. H. Racker, *Transference and Countertransference.*

41. Jung, "The Psychology of the Transference," CW 16, pars. 364ff.

42. See Otto Kernberg, *Borderline Conditions and Pathological Narcissism.*

43. See Mario Jacoby, "Reflections on Heinz Kohut's Concept of Narcissism," and Nathan Schwartz-Salant, *Narcissism and Character Transformation.*

44. Heinz Kohut, *The Restoration of the Self,* p. 255.

45. E. Barmeyer, *Die Musen.*

46. The psychology of these early maturational phases has been, and still is, a subject of much lively discussion and controversy. See, for example, Michael Fordham, *Children as Individuals* and *The Self and Autism;* R. Ledermann, "Narcissistic Disorder and Its Treatment"; and M.S. Mahler, *The Psychological Birth of the Human Infant.* Also Erich Neumann, *The Child,* and Joseph Chilton Pearce, *Magical Child.*

47. Heinz Kohut, *The Analysis of the Self.*

48. Kernberg, *Borderline Conditions.*

49. D.W. Winnicott, "Psychiatric Disorder in Terms of Infantile Maturational Processes," p. 24.

50. Kohut, *The Restoration of the Self.*

51. See Lambert, *Analysis, Repair and Individuation,* p. 142; and Fordham, *Jungian Psychotherapy.*

52. J. MacQuarrie, *Twentieth-Century Religious Thought,* p. 196.

53. Neumann, *The Child.*

54. Rosemary Gordon, "Transference as a Fulcrum of Analysis," p. 116.

55. Jung, *The Visions Seminars,* p. 506.

56. Jung, "The Psychology of the Transference," CW 16, par. 374.

57. Jung, *Psychological Types,* CW 6, par. 784.

58. Jung, "The Tavistock Lectures," CW 18, pars. 368ff.

59. Jung, "New Paths in Psychology," in *Two Essays on Analytical Psychology,* CW 7, par. 409.

60. Jung, "The Psychology of the Transference," CW 16, par. 386.

61. Ibid., par. 381.

62. See A. Guggenbühl-Craig, *Power in the Helping Professions.*

63. Jung, "The Psychology of the Transference," CW 16, par. 538.

64. Ibid., pars. 381, 410.

65. Ibid., par. 469.

66. Ibid., pars. 448-449.

Glossary of Jungian Terms

Anima (Latin, "soul"). The unconscious, feminine side of a man's personality. She is personified in dreams by images of women ranging from prostitute and seductress to spiritual guide (Wisdom). She is the eros principle, hence a man's anima development is reflected in how he relates to women. Identification with the anima can appear as moodiness, effeminacy, and oversensitivity. Jung calls the anima *the archetype of life itself.*

Animus (Latin, "spirit"). The unconscious, masculine side of a woman's personality. He personifies the logos principle. Identification with the animus can cause a woman to become rigid, opinionated, and argumentative. More positively, he is the inner man who acts as a bridge between the woman's ego and her own creative resources in the unconscious.

Archetypes. Irrepresentable in themselves, but their effects appear in consciousness as the archetypal images and ideas. These are universal patterns or motifs which come from the collective unconscious and are the basic content of religions, mythologies, legends, and fairytales. They emerge in individuals through dreams and visions.

Association. A spontaneous flow of interconnected thoughts and images around a specific idea, determined by unconscious connections.

Complex. An emotionally charged group of ideas or images. At the "center" of a complex is an archetype or archetypal image.

Constellate. Whenever there is a strong emotional reaction to a person or a situation, a complex has been constellated (activated).

Ego. The central complex in the field of consciousness. A strong ego can relate objectively to activated contents of the unconscious (i.e., other complexes), rather than identifying with them, which appears as a state of possession.

Feeling. One of the four psychic functions. It is a rational function which evaluates the worth of relationships and situations. Feeling must be distinguished from emotion, which is due to an activated complex.

Individuation. The conscious realization of one's unique psychological reality, including both strengths and limitations. It leads to the experience of the Self as the regulating center of the psyche.

Inflation. A state in which one has an unrealistically high or low (negative inflation) sense of identity. It indicates a regression of consciousness into unconsciousness, which typically happens when the ego takes too many unconscious contents upon itself and loses the faculty of discrimination.

Intuition. One of the four psychic functions. It is the irrational function which tells us the possibilities inherent in the present. In contrast to sensation (the function which perceives immediate reality through the physical senses) intuition perceives via the unconscious, e.g., flashes of insight of unknown origin.

Participation mystique. A term derived from the anthropologist Lévy-Bruhl, denoting a primitive, psychological connection with objects, or between persons, resulting in a strong unconscious bond.

Persona (Latin, "actor's mask"). One's social role, derived from the expectations of society and early training. A strong ego relates to the outside world through a flexible persona; identification with a specific persona (doctor, scholar, artist, etc.) inhibits psychological development.

Projection. The process whereby an unconscious quality or characteristic of one's own is perceived and reacted to in an outer object or person. Projection of the anima or animus onto a real women or man is experienced as falling in love. Frustrated expectations indicate the need to withdraw projections, in order to relate to the reality of other people.

Puer aeternus (Latin, "eternal youth"). Indicates a certain type of man who remains too long in adolescent psychology, generally associated with a strong unconscious attachment to the mother (actual or symbolic). Positive traits are spontaneity and openness to change. His female counterpart is the **puella,** an "eternal girl" with a corresponding attachment to the father-world.

Self. The archetype of wholeness and the regulating center of the personality. It is experienced as a transpersonal power which transcends the ego, e.g., God.

Senex (Latin, "old man"). Associated with attitudes that come with advancing age. Negatively, this can mean cynicism, rigidity and extreme conservatism; positive traits are responsibility, orderliness and self-discipline. A well-balanced personality functions appropriately within the puer-senex polarity.

Shadow. An unconscious part of the personality characterized by traits and attitudes, whether negative or positive, which the conscious ego tends to reject or ignore. It is personified in dreams by persons of the same sex as the dreamer. Consciously assimilating one's shadow usually results in an increase of energy.

Symbol. The best possible expression for something essentially unknown. Symbolic thinking is non-linear, right-brain oriented; it is complementary to logical, linear, left-brain thinking.

Transcendent function. The reconciling "third" which emerges from the unconscious (in the form of a symbol or a new attitude) after the conflicting opposites have been consciously differentiated, and the tension between them held.

Transference and countertransference. Particular cases of projection, commonly used to describe the unconscious, emotional bonds that arise between two persons in an analytic or therapeutic relationship.

Uroboros. The mythical snake or dragon that eats its own tail. It is a symbol both for individuation as a self-contained, circular process, and for narcissistic self-absorption.

Bibliography

Adler, G., and A. Jaffé, eds. *C.G. Jung Letters* (Bollingen Series XCV). 2 vols. Princeton University Press, Princeton, 1975.

Barmeyer, E. *Die Musen* (Humanistische Bibliothek, Reihe 1, Band 2). Fink, Munich, 1968.

Blomeyer, R. "Die Konstellierung der Gegenübertragung beim Auftreten archetypischer Träume." *Zeitschrift für analytische Psychologie*, vol. 3.

Buber, M. *I and Thou*. Trans. Walter Kaufmann. Scribner, New York, 1970.

Dieckmann, H. "Die Konstellierung der Gegenübertragung beim Auftreten archetypischer Träume." *Zeitschrift für analytische Psychologie*, vol. 3.

Erikson, E.H. *Childhood and Society*. W.W. Norton and Co., New York, 1950.

Fordham, M. *Children as Individuals*. Hodder & Stoughton, London, 1969.

————. *The Self and Autism* (Library of Analytical Psychology, vol. 3). Heinemann, London, 1976.

————. *Jungian Psychotherapy*. John Wiley and Sons, Chichester, 1978.

————, et al. *Technique in Jungian Analysis* (Library of Analytical Psychology, vol. 2). Heinemann, London, 1974.

Freud, S. *The Complete Psychological Works of Sigmund Freud*. Ed. James Strachey. The Hogarth Press and the Institute of Psychoanalysis, London, 1978.

Gordon, R. "Transference as a Fulcrum of Analysis." *Journal of Analytical Psychology*, vol. 13, no. 2 (July 1968).

Guggenbühl-Craig, A. *Power in the Helping Professions*. Spring Publications, Zurich, 1978.

Hall, James. *Jungian Dream Interpretation: A Handbook of Theory and Practice*. Inner City Books, Toronto, 1983.

Heimann, P. "On Countertransference." *International Journal of Psychoanalysis*, vol. 31 (1950).

Jacoby, M. "A Contribution to the Phenomenon of Transference." *Journal of Analytical Psychology*, vol. 14, no. 2 (July 1969).

————. "Reflections on Heinz Kohut's Concept of Narcissism." *Journal of Analytical Psychology*, vol. 26, no. 4 (October 1981).

119

Jones, E. *Sigmund Freud: Life and Work.* Hogarth Press, London, 1953.

Jung, C.G. *The Collected Works* (Bollingen Series XX). 20 vols. Trans. R.F.C. Hull, Ed. H. Read, M. Fordham, G. Adler, Wm. McGuire. Princeton University Press, Princeton, 1953-1979.

———. *The Visions Seminars.* Spring Publications, Zürich, 1976.

Kernberg, O.F. *Borderline Conditions and Pathological Narcissism.* Adonson, New York, 1975.

Kohut, H. *The Analysis of the Self.* International Universities Press, New York, 1971.

———. *The Restoration of the Self.* International Universities Press, New York, 1977.

Lambert, K. *Analysis, Repair and Individuation* (Library of Analytical Psychology, vol. 5). Academic Press, London, 1981.

MacQuarrie, J. *Twentieth-Century Religious Thought.* SCM Press, London, 1963.

Mahler, M.S. *The Psychological Birth of the Human Infant.* Basic Books, New York, 1975.

Neumann, E. *Zur Psychologie des Weiblichen.* Rascher, Zürich, 1953.

———. *The Child.* Putnam, New York, 1973.

Pearce, J.C. *Magical Child.* E.P. Dutton, New York, 1977.

Racker, H. *Transference and Countertransference.* Hogarth Press, London, 1968.

Reich, A. "On Countertransference." *International Journal of Psychoanalysis,* vol. 32 (1951).

Schwartz-Salant, Nathan. *Narcissism and Character Transformation: The Psychology of Narcissistic Character Disorders.* Inner City Books, Toronto, 1982.

Von Franz, Marie-Louise. *Alchemy: An Introduction to the Symbolism and the Psychology.* Inner City Books, Toronto, 1980.

Willi, J. *Die Zweierbeziehung.* Rohwolt, Reinbek b. Hamburg, 1975.

Winnicott, D.W. "Psychiatric Disorder in Terms of Infantile Maturational Processes." *The Maturational Processes and the Facilitating Environment.* International Universities Press, New York, 1965.

Index

121

Studies in Jungian Psychology
by Jungian Analysts

Quality Paperbacks

Prices and payment in $US (in Canada, $Cdn)

1. The Secret Raven: Conflict and Transformation
Daryl Sharp (Toronto). ISBN 0-919123-00-7. 128 pp. $15

2. The Psychological Meaning of Redemption Motifs in Fairy Tales
Marie-Louise von Franz (Zurich). ISBN 0-919123-01-5. 128 pp. $15

3. On Divination and Synchronicity: The Psychology of Meaningful Chance Marie-Louise von Franz (Zurich). ISBN 0-919123-02-3. 128 pp. $15

4. The Owl Was a Baker's Daughter: Obesity, Anorexia and the Repressed Feminine M. Woodman (Toronto). ISBN 0-919123-03-1. 144 pp. $16

5. Alchemy: An Introduction to the Symbolism and the Psychology
Marie-Louise von Franz (Zurich). ISBN 0-919123-04-X. 288 pp. $18

6. Descent to the Goddess: A Way of Initiation for Women
Sylvia Brinton Perera (New York). ISBN 0-919123-05-8. 112 pp. $15

7. The Psyche as Sacrament: A Comparative Study of C.G. Jung and Paul Tillich John P. Dourley (Ottawa). ISBN 0-919123-06-6. 128 pp. $15

8. Border Crossings: Carlos Castaneda's Path of Knowledge
Donald Lee Williams (Boulder). ISBN 0-919123-07-4. 160 pp. $16

9. Narcissism and Character Transformation: The Psychology of Narcissistic Character Disorders
Nathan Schwartz-Salant (New York). ISBN 0-919123-08-2. 192 pp. $18

10. Rape and Ritual: A Psychological Study
Bradley A. Te Paske (Minneapolis). ISBN 0-919123-09-0. 160 pp. $16

11. Alcoholism and Women: The Background and the Psychology
Jan Bauer (Montreal). ISBN 0-919123-10-4. 144 pp. $16

12. Addiction to Perfection: The Still Unravished Bride
Marion Woodman (Toronto). ISBN 0-919123-11-2. 208 pp. $18pb/$20hc

13. Jungian Dream Interpretation: A Handbook of Theory and Practice
James A. Hall, M.D. (Dallas). ISBN 0-919123-12-0. 128 pp. $15

14. The Creation of Consciousness: Jung's Myth for Modern Man
Edward F. Edinger (Los Angeles). ISBN 0-919123-13-9. 128 pp. $15

15. The Analytic Encounter: Transference and Human Relationship
Mario Jacoby (Zurich). ISBN 0-919123-14-7. 128 pp. $15

16. Change of Life: Dreams and the Menopause
Ann Mankowitz (Santa Fe). ISBN 0-919123-15-5. 128 pp. $15

17. The Illness That We Are: A Jungian Critique of Christianity
John P. Dourley (Ottawa). ISBN 0-919123-16-3. 128 pp. $15

18. Hags and Heroes: A Feminist Approach to Jungian Psychotherapy with Couples P. Young-Eisendrath (Philadelphia). ISBN 0-919123-17-1. 192 pp. $18

19. Cultural Attitudes in Psychological Perspective
Joseph L. Henderson, M.D. (San Francisco). ISBN 0-919123-18-X. 128 pp. $15

20. The Vertical Labyrinth: Individuation in Jungian Psychology
Aldo Carotenuto (Rome). ISBN 0-919123-19-8. 144 pp. $16

21. The Pregnant Virgin: A Process of Psychological Transformation
Marion Woodman (Toronto). ISBN 0-919123-20-1. 208 pp. $18pb/$20hc

22. Encounter with the Self: A Jungian Commentary on William Blake's
Illustrations of the Book of Job
Edward F. Edinger (Los Angeles). ISBN 0-919123-21-X. 80 pp. $12

23. The Scapegoat Complex: Toward a Mythology of Shadow and Guilt
Sylvia Brinton Perera (New York). ISBN 0-919123-22-8. 128 pp. $15

24. The Bible and the Psyche: Individuation Symbolism in the Old
Testament   Edward F. Edinger (Los Angeles). ISBN 0-919123-23-6. 176 pp. $18

25. The Spiral Way: A Woman's Healing Journey
Aldo Carotenuto (Rome). ISBN 0-919123-24-4. 144 pp. $16

26. The Jungian Experience: Analysis and Individuation
James A. Hall, M.D. (Dallas). ISBN 0-919123-25-2. 176 pp. $18

27. Phallos: Sacred Image of the Masculine
Eugene Monick (Scranton/New York). ISBN 0-919123-26-0. 144 pp. $16

28. The Christian Archetype: A Jungian Commentary on the Life of
Christ   Edward F. Edinger (Los Angeles). ISBN 0-919123-27-9. 144 pp. $16

29. Love, Celibacy and the Inner Marriage
John P. Dourley (Ottawa). ISBN 0-919123-28-7. 128 pp. $15

30. Touching: Body Therapy and Depth Psychology
Deldon Anne McNeely (Lynchburg, VA). ISBN 0-919123-29-5. 128 pp. $15

31. Personality Types: Jung's Model of Typology
Daryl Sharp (Toronto). ISBN 0-919123-30-9. 128 pp. $15

32. The Sacred Prostitute: Eternal Aspect of the Feminine
Nancy Qualls-Corbett (Birmingham). ISBN 0-919123-31-7. 176 pp. $18

33. When the Spirits Come Back
Janet O. Dallett (Seal Harbor, WA). ISBN 0-919123-32-5. 160 pp. $16

34. The Mother: Archetypal Image in Fairy Tales
Sibylle Birkhäuser-Oeri (Zurich). ISBN 0-919123-33-3. 176 pp. $18

35. The Survival Papers: Anatomy of a Midlife Crisis
Daryl Sharp (Toronto). ISBN 0-919123-34-1. 160 pp. $15

36. The Cassandra Complex: Living with Disbelief
Laurie Layton Schapira (New York). ISBN 0-919123-35-X. 160 pp. $16

37. Dear Gladys: The Survival Papers, Book 2
Daryl Sharp (Toronto). ISBN 0-919123-36-8.   144 pp. $15

38. The Phallic Quest: Priapus and Masculine Inflation
James Wyly (Chicago). ISBN 0-919123-37-6. 128 pp. $15

39. Acrobats of the Gods: Dance and Transformation
Joan Dexter Blackmer (Concord, MA). ISBN 0-919123-38-4. 128 pp. $15

40. Eros and Pathos: Shades of Love and Suffering
Aldo Carotenuto (Rome). ISBN 0-919123-39-2. 160 pp. $16

41. The Ravaged Bridegroom: Masculinity in Women
Marion Woodman (Toronto). ISBN 0-919123-42-2. 224 pp. $18

42. Liberating the Heart: Spirituality and Jungian Psychology
Lawrence W. Jaffe (Berkeley). ISBN 0-919123-43-0. 176 pp. $18

43. Goethe's *Faust:* Notes for a Jungian Commentary
Edward F. Edinger (Los Angeles). ISBN 0-919123-44-9. 112 pp. $15

Add Postage/Handling: 1-2 books, $2; 3-4 books, $4; 5-8 books, $7

INNER CITY BOOKS, Box 1271, Station Q,
Toronto, ON M4T 2P4, Canada
Tel. (416) 927-0355   *Fax (416) 924-1814*